B
FOLEY

Bennett, A

The cost of

$26.00

DATE			
AG 1 1 '12			
SE 1 9 '12			
OC 0 5 '12			
NO 2 2 '12			
DE 1 1 '12			
JA 0 3 '13			

The Cost of Hope

The Cost of Hope

A MEMOIR

Amanda Bennett

RANDOM HOUSE
New York

Published in the United States by Random House, an imprint
of The Random House Publishing Group, a division of Random
House, Inc., New York.

RANDOM HOUSE and colophon are registered trademarks of
Random House, Inc.

Bennett, Amanda.
The cost of hope : a memoir / Amanda Bennett.
p. cm.
Includes bibliographical references.
ISBN 978-1-4000-6984-2
eBook ISBN 978-0-679-60484-6
1. Foley, Terence Bryan—Health. 2. Cancer—Patients—
Biography. I. Title.
RC265.6.F65B46 2012
362.196'9940092—dc23
[B]   2011040660

Printed in the United States of America on acid-free paper

www.atrandom.com

2 4 6 8 9 7 5 3 1

FIRST EDITION

Book Design by Simon M. Sullivan

For Terry and Georgia

The Cost of Hope

Prologue

The foreign correspondent's apartment not far from mine in Peking is warm with music and laughter. It is Saturday, September 3, 1983, and I have been working here as the lone *Wall Street Journal* reporter for more than seven months. Tonight, a story I am trying to write will not be tamed. Frustration has chained me to my typewriter late into the night, and now I am looking for some diversion.

There is so little to do in China at night that any party is a magnet, not just for newspeople, but for the diplomats and businesspeople who are every bit as isolated and lonely as we are. At any party you are as likely to find wildcatters as bankers, and diplomats from Bali, Paris, and Manila mixing with journalists from Bombay and Madrid. The Africans mainly socialize among themselves, as do most of the Japanese. But every other nationality and profession mixes indiscriminately on any occasion.

I step in from the darkness.

Everyone is dressed to relax, in jeans, shirts, and ratty sweaters. I am wearing my usual work outfit of sweatpants and a shirt two sizes too big. Over on the sofa, though, the guy with a drink in one hand and a cigarette in the other is wearing a gray three-piece suit. And a bow tie. A bow tie! The person sitting next to him gets up to leave. Before I can look away, Mr. Bow Tie beckons me to the empty seat.

By way of conversation with a stranger, I explain what I am doing there, and about the story that is stumping me, the one that has kept me at my desk so late on a Saturday night. Terence Foley turns out to be an expert on the very subject I am working on. Not just an expert, but a witty one. Erudite. Almost dazzlingly articulate. Who is this man? And what marvelous stroke of luck has landed me next to him at the moment I need him?

We talk so intently that we barely notice the party is winding down and the other guests are drifting off into the near dawn.

Twenty-four years later, in the intensive care ward at the University of Pennsylvania hospital, Dr. Eric Goren tells me Terence, my husband of twenty years, may not live till morning.

It is sometime after midnight on December 8, 2007. Terence Bryan Foley, sixty-seven years old, Mr. Bow Tie, father of our two teenagers, a Chinese historian who earned his Ph.D. in his sixties, a man who plays more than fifteen musical instruments and speaks six languages, a San Francisco cable car conductor and sports photographer, an expert on dairy cattle and swine nutrition, film noir and Dixieland jazz, is confused. He knows his name but not the year. He wants a Coke.

Should Terence begin to hemorrhage, the doctor asks, what should he do?

It's the kind of question medical professionals like Dr. Goren and families like ours face every day. Can we—should we—prolong this beloved person's life? For a few days? A few weeks? If we are lucky, for longer?

This is Terence's and my third end-of-life warning. We've won seven years. Can we get more?

Dr. Keith Flaherty and I both believe—hope—that a new medicine Terence has just begun to take will buy him more time.

Keep him alive if you can, I say. Let's see what this new drug can do.

What I couldn't know then was that the thinking behind my

request—keep him alive if you can—along with hundreds of decisions we made over seven years, would illustrate the impossible calculus at the core of life, of love of family, and of the U.S. health care debate.

Backed by medical insurance provided by my corporate employers, we were able to fight for Terence's life with a series of expensive last chances like the one I asked for that night.

How expensive?

When I finally knew, the bills totaled $618,616, almost two-thirds of it for the final twenty-four months. Most of the money was for treatments that no one can say for sure helped extend his life.

This is not the tragic story of a family denied care for lack of resources, or of the struggles of the more than 46 million uninsured Americans. Quite the contrary. Our insurance coverage gave us access to the best medical care all across the country. It isn't our children's story either. Terry, now twenty-two, and Georgia, now seventeen, were at the center of everything throughout. It is for them especially that Terence wanted to live on. In this book, though, they play only cameo roles. I have their permission to tell their dad's story, and mine. I do not have their permission to tell theirs. They were children when most of this story took place and teens when their dad died. They are protective of their thoughts and feelings and their relationship with him; I am protective of their privacy. Perhaps someday they will want to tell their own stories. This, however, is not that story.

Instead, this is about Terence and me. About the choices we made. It is about a marriage and love. About a man and his life. It's about family and everything we did to try to save the husband and father at the core of it. It is also the story of how I set about to understand, after Terence died, why I did what I did, why the doctors did what they did, and why Terence did what he did—and to try to find out the cost of hope.

1

It almost always begins in darkness, my memory's trip back to the China where Terence and I meet.

In the first week of February 1983, I fly in to Peking to take up my post as the correspondent for *The Wall Street Journal.* I am looking out the window of a Pan Am flight as it circles, preparing to land. Below is the country's capital, one of the world's biggest cities. This is not the China of the Olympics, the futuristic seventy-story towers and magnetic trains, of stylish wealthy entrepreneurs and world-devouring currency reserves. In 1983, eleven years after President Nixon's 1972 walk along the Great Wall, the country is still enmeshed in the shock and trauma of the Cultural Revolution and of the turbulent three decades since the People's Republic of China was formed in 1949. It's still easy to see the gashing wounds from years of isolation, poverty, and the political instability of the Cultural Revolution that has barely ended.

Peking—it is still Peking in those days—is the home of 9.3 million people, yet there is none of the exuberant burst of light that normally greets travelers flying into a big city. There are no ocher ribbons of highway spiraling out from the city's center, nor do snakes of white headlights flow in one direction, red taillights in another. No massive office buildings flaunt shining squares into the night long after the workers have left for home. There are no cheerfully lighted houses either, no boxlike warrens of high-rise apartments fanning out to lighted loops of suburban cul-de-sacs.

Instead, here in China's capital in the early 1980s, most people still live in dark one-story brick or stone courtyard houses with public street latrines. Even in the center of the city, some families still raise chickens and small pigs. Many homes still have no electricity at all.

It is a dark and silent city. In 1983 the country still hasn't recovered from the decadelong nightmare of the Cultural Revolution that pitted colleague against colleague, neighbor against neighbor, child against parent. The bleakness disturbs me. There are only a handful of cars—some owned by a tiny city-owned taxi fleet, a few driven by diplomats or journalists, as well as the hulking Russian-style Hongqi limousines favored by high-ranking Party officials. Someone sometime told someone that headlights burn gasoline, so only parking lights are used at night. The cars are ghostly shadows with tiny yellow cats' eyes.

Almost all the necessities of life—food, clothing, shelter—are supplied by the factory or office. Stores have only recently begun to reemerge, but most shop windows are still boarded up or plastered over. For many weeks I don't even realize that these darkened doorways are stores. It is a dingy, featureless wasteland.

For the first several months I live alone in an apartment that is also my office. While the telex clatters behind me, every night I stand on the twelfth-floor balcony looking down into the dark night toward the southeast of the city. I live herded together with the other journalists and diplomats in this walled compound of cinder-block buildings, guarded—and watched—by soldiers.

The winter air is bitter with the smoke of the soft coal briquettes that people use to heat their houses. Off in the distance I hear the wail of a train whistle. Directly below me, metal clops against asphalt as the horse-drawn delivery carts still allowed into the center city after sundown make their nightly rounds. Even late at night the streets pulse with bikers heading to work or back home or who knows where. Only the barest hint of color—

a sleeve, a scarf, a ribbon—has begun to appear here and there to brighten the Communist-era Mao-style dress. Otherwise the bikers, both men and women, are all dark. Dark jackets. Dark trousers. Dark shoes. Dark hats. Dark bikes.

I stand on my balcony and think how lucky I am to be here at this historic moment—how excited, and at the same time how frightened, alone, and confused I am in this bleak, strange, unwelcoming place.

On Saturday, September 3, 1983, as midnight approaches I am still working. I work pretty much all the time. Just as I am starting to fade with exhaustion, New York wakes up with its barrage of questions and comments and demands. Working all day and then answering the phone through the night adds a kind of surreal, never-quite-awake/never-quite-asleep quality to my life in China.

Tonight I struggle with the story that just won't fall into shape. Mikhail Kapitsa, a Soviet deputy foreign minister, is set to arrive in the capital. He is the highest-ranking Soviet to visit since China and the Soviet Union broke off relations in 1960. Because the two countries had split, few Soviet experts are left in China, at least ones willing to talk. I can find almost no one who understands the politics of both countries well enough to explain the significance of the visit. There is no Internet; I check the indexes of all the reference books I have brought and find nothing. My interviews have been next to useless.

I planned to skip the party that John Broder, the *Chicago Tribune* correspondent, is throwing. I must get this piece written! But I am worn out, lonely, and discouraged. I leave the yellow sheets in the typewriter and wander over, intending to stay for only a few minutes. John Broder is a witty, lively, guitar-playing bon vivant. His wife is beautiful and dark-haired with a wisp of an exotic accent—Israeli? Their party is an event.

The bow-tied man on the sofa across the room is wearing

horn-rimmed glasses. He looks a bit out of place, maybe even a bit out of time. He's older than the others. Stouter. More formal.

When he motions me over, I settle in next to him and begin to tell him the subject of my troublesome story. His eyes light up. Sino-Soviet politics are his specialty, he says. In fact, he is here in Peking as a Fulbright scholar, on a one-year fellowship to China precisely to study the relations between China and the Soviet Union. We begin an intense conversation about the personal and professional hostilities between Mao and Stalin that had led to the countries' rift in the 1950s. The terrible economic price China had paid for the split. The effect on world politics of the two rivals, and the change in balance of power when the United States opened its arms gingerly again to China. It is a masterful discussion. Just what I have been missing. Just what I need. I am not so much of a geek as to bring a notepad to the party, so I try to memorize as much as I can before, close to 3:00 a.m., I say good night and walk home alone. I live only two buildings over, inside the compound surrounded by soldiers. By the next morning I remember the substance of the talk but not the man's name.

That afternoon I call our host. The Fulbright scholar? John is stumped. People just show up at his parties. He didn't know half the people in the room. I make a few other calls, but no one seems to recall the proper middle-aged man with the owlish glasses and bow tie. Without a name to pin the observations on, I'm not comfortable writing the story, so I let it go and chalk it up as another disappointment.

A few months go by. I have almost forgotten about him in the press of work. Then, without warning, I spot him again at another staple of 1980s China social life—a bank reception. A big American bank is opening its office here. It has rented the courtyard of a lovely old prerevolutionary home. The space is filled with the usual assortment of businesspeople, journalists, and Chinese officials in Mao jackets. There are drinks and hors d'oeuvres and endless speeches about friendship and cooperation. He is standing alone.

"I've been looking for you," I say.

"I was going to call," he answers. "I've been traveling." This time, at a business occasion instead of a party, he automatically hands me his card, as I just as automatically hold out mine.

TERENCE B. FOLEY
COUNTRY DIRECTOR
AMERICAN SOYBEAN ASSOCIATION

"Soybeans? I don't understand. You said you were a Fulbright scholar. Studying Sino-Soviet relations."

He shrugs. "You're cute. You're a journalist. I wanted to talk to you. Journalists are always working. How long would you have talked to me if I told you I was in soybeans? You wanted to talk about China and Russia, so I made up a person who could talk about China and Russia. I knew you'd find out sooner or later."

Soybeans?

Made it up?

I stare at the card.

"You asshole!" I finally blurt out. "You could have gotten me fired!" I stamp away.

And that is how we met.

Years later, this becomes our signature story, a kind of stand-up routine for both of us. When our children are old enough, we tell them the story at least once a year.

At his funeral, I stand up and tell it alone.

I don't see him again until about three months later, on February 2, 1984. It's Chinese New Year, the first day of the Year of the

Rat. I spot him in a boarding lounge in Tokyo, both of us heading back to the city that by now has been renamed Beijing. I'm on my way back from my first home leave. He's coming back from who knows where. He is in business class and doesn't see me turning right into coach.

There aren't more than a dozen people in the cavernous rear of the plane. All commerce and diplomatic work stops for the New Year holiday, and no sane tourist goes to frigid, polluted Beijing in February, which a colleague once described as like being stuck inside a vacuum cleaner bag inside a freezer. Exhausted from a full day of upright flying back from my leave in New York, I lie down across three seats and fall asleep.

When we arrive in Beijing at midnight, the airport is more dreary than usual. Even in broad daylight the Beijing airport is a depressing place, cold and barren and more like a military hangar than a modern commercial airport. Even at its bustling peak, there is no food. No publicly available phones. In those days before cellphones, once inside the airport, you were nearly cut off from the rest of the world.

Tonight, the baggage handlers sullenly fling the bags onto the wooden pallets. Eager to get home for the holiday, skinny pig-tailed girls wearing khaki green airport service uniforms scurry around flipping off light switches even before the plane is fully unloaded. I look around. The few people on the plane have been met by relatives, or by their work units, or by their drivers. My own driver is home with his family. I gave him the holiday off, thinking taxis would certainly be available. Tonight there are none. It is minus 14 degrees Celsius—not even 7 degrees Fahrenheit. There is an eighteen-mile-long deserted road fringed with linden trees between me and home.

Then I spot him over by a service desk, a telephone in his hand. He is a hefty man but even across the room he looks oddly puffed up like Santa Claus, a navy greatcoat ballooning around him. He has found an airport telephone tucked inside a service desk. I give him points for that. Still, I feel a faint wave of contempt. Of course he is going to need me to help him translate. I am no expert, but I have quickly made myself functional in the language. Older American businessmen, in my experience, have not.

I start across the room to offer to help, when a sudden torrent of rapid-fire, colloquial Chinese bursts out of him. He speaks so fast I can't understand anything he says. He hangs up the phone and turns to me.

"I live in a hotel," he says. "I've asked the desk to send a car to get us."

Us?

I see I really haven't much of a choice. We are the only two passengers left in the airport, and the last of the lights are going out. As we wait for the car, I watch in amazement as he begins pulling videotapes out from every wrinkle in his clothing. He is smoking, talking, and unloading all at once. His outside pockets. Inside pockets. Pants pockets. Inside his bloused-out shirt. His front waistband. His rear waistband. Altogether he stacks more than twenty cassettes that he had just smuggled in. *The Quiet Man. All About Eve. Apocalypse Now. Lawrence of Arabia. The Man Who Shot Liberty Valance. The Maltese Falcon. Vertigo. The Big Sleep. Dr. Strangelove. Bonnie and Clyde. Top Hat.* They are all classics, and they aren't illegal. It's just that bored officials with no other entertainment have a habit of taking videos to check for subversive material and then "losing" them.

"I have more than five hundred movies in my apartment," he boasts. "I tape them off TV in the U.S. and bring them in every trip."

Despite his grin, it is clear that I was wrong in supposing that he hadn't noticed me boarding. He is peevish.

"I tried to talk to you the whole plane ride home. I kept walking back and all I saw was your feet."

"I was asleep."

"I went back a whole bunch of times and all there was to talk to was Mel Searls." Mel is the portly and kindly U.S. embassy commercial counselor. This is obviously my fault.

"I was asleep," I repeat.

"I like Mel, but I can't talk to him for five hours."

"I WAS ASLEEP." This guy is ticking me off.

"So now what's going to happen is you're going to come back to my place and we will watch a movie, have a drink, and eat some treats."

Uh, I think, that is not even close to what is going to happen. I am going to go home to bed. Alone.

Jet lag is my only explanation for what comes next. It is 1:00 a.m. in Beijing, but my body thinks it is 1:00 p.m. in New York. On the drive home I confront the reality that back at my miserable apartment I will face at least six terrible hours in my empty cinderblock office/home standing on the balcony unable to sleep but unable to do much else either. So when the car pulls up to my door—the soldier waved us past when he saw the white faces inside—I drop my luggage in the apartment and rejoin him.

He lives down the road in the Jianguo Hotel, the first new hotel built in China since the 1950s. It is a joint venture modeled on a California Holiday Inn and it is a foreigners' oasis, with new carpets, polite staff, a private supply of salad greens grown without benefit of human manure, and a small restaurant serving hamburgers. Journalists and diplomats live in compounds. Businesspeople live in hotels. He has scored the Jianguo, the only one of its kind in China.

He opens the door to his home, a seventeen-by-seventeen room downstairs with a few steps leading to another room the same size upstairs. It is a standard-issue Holiday Inn hotel room, complete with a painting over the sofa of birches reflected in a pond. Except for one thing: It is stuffed like a warehouse from top to bottom. He opens the door to the downstairs half bath. It can no longer be used as a bath, as it is packed tight to the ceiling with labeled boxes. There are boxes reading "Videos: Classic"; "Videos: Japanese"; "Videos: Christmas"; "Videos: Film Noir/Detective/Crime." He files away his latest stash. I see boxes of Christmas decorations and what appears to be a full-size artificial Christmas tree swathed in plastic. There are boxes labeled "Halloween" and "Fourth of July." There is a flagpole and large American flag, a dart board, a badminton set. There are musical instruments. A banjo. A small tuba. There are boxes marked "cameras," "darkroom equipment," and "entomology." I can see insect nets and tracing paper and huge aluminum-shrouded lights, the kind used in those days for lighting close-ups. There are games. Monopoly. Parcheesi. Backgammon. In the spare, featureless, empty landscape of Beijing, his room assaults my senses.

Upstairs, his bedroom can barely be called a bedroom. The standard-issue Holiday Inn king is the only bare spot. He has constructed bookshelves and packed them with books in, as far as I can tell, at least six languages. One whole set of shelves is devoted to cooking gear. A clearly unapproved hot plate. Saucepans. Frying pans. A Dutch oven. Whisks and slotted spoons, wooden spatulas and pancake turners. A waffle iron. Boxes and boxes of cake mix and canned fruit, cans of cinnamon and sugar and vanilla and cocoa powder and garlic salt. He also has a full set of barware, shot glasses and tumblers and martini glasses, a shaker, narrow-mouthed white-wine glasses and wide-bowled red-wine glasses, beer steins with handles, an ice bucket with tongs, and tall glasses for gin and tonic.

I pick a demure Drambuie from a shelf crammed with every form of wine, liquor, and liqueur imaginable—all in tiny, one-serving airline bottles. Clearly this is a man who does a lot of flying. He pours out a dish of mixed nuts and one of cookies, both hand-carried in from home. "Treats!" he says. We settle in to watch *Tom Jones*.

By the end of the movie the sun is coming up. We have barely spoken. I try to make conversation but it is plain that there is a right way and a wrong way to watch movies with Mr. Foley. Total silence and concentration is the right way. Any kind of distracting small talk is the wrong way. I stand to go. He walks over and stands facing me. Here it comes, I think. Then he reaches past me and pulls a map of China from one of the shelves. He is suddenly all business, and talking rapidly.

"So here is what we are going to do." It isn't a question.

"There are seventeen cities we're allowed to visit now. Over the next couple of years there will be more. If we start now, we can get to all of them by the time our tour is up. You're probably here for what—two, three years? If I need to, I can extend my tour. So can you, I suppose, if we need to. There's Kunming, Chongqing, Chengdu, Wuhan..." He begins rattling off the names of Chinese cities.

"We'll travel all over China together. We've got to start right away. We haven't got that much time. You are going to be somebody. You're going to need somebody to take care of you. We'll see everything we can in China. Then we'll get married in the Great Hall of the People—I think they are letting foreigners get married there now—but anyway, we can get married again back home, and then we'll have a raft of kids. We have to get moving."

Who is this guy? What is he saying? Did he just ask me to marry him? Oddly enough, it is his phrasing that strikes me first. A raft of kids? Who says "raft"? For that matter, who says "treats"? Who proposes to a woman he doesn't know—who clearly is hostile to him—after one evening watching movies together? This guy is out of his mind. I thank him for the movie and the drink and leave, intending that this meeting be our last.

. . .

The next day, I find myself climbing Coal Hill with him. From the top of the hill, behind the Forbidden City, wrapped up against the razor wind, we can see down into the Imperial Palace and across the city. The next day, another movie. Then a tour around Tiananmen Square. Then dinner. Then a night in his room, then a night in mine. Soon he is writing his reports after midnight at my interpreter's desk while I struggle to get a story through the balky telex machine. And I am setting up a portable typewriter on a TV table in his bedroom.

Why do I keep meeting with this man? At forty-four, he's twelve years older than I am. He's chubby. No, he's overweight. He wears owl glasses and bow ties. He's crazy. And we're angry with each other almost twenty-four hours a day.

Probably the searing loneliness of our surroundings has something to do with it. I have been here only a little more than a year and the tension of the aloneness is already close to breaking me. It is a different kind of loneliness than I have ever experienced, a kind of black hole that pulls me down as if underwater and often ends in panic. He feels it too. He has been here for more than three years already, and he tells me about long nights sitting immobile on the edge of his bed, his head in his hands, or pacing the room frantically, so fiercely lonely he believes he will go mad.

Visitors nod sagely. Of course it is hard. There are no movies or bookstores or symphonies or bars. No cereal, or familiar shampoo, or drinkable tap water or Tampax. A handful of places serve what passes for Western food, but it is just familiar enough to spark loneliness, not satisfaction. Yes, the tourists say pityingly; they understand.

The truth is, they understand nothing. Nothing about the lack of creature comforts really matters. We can live without hamburgers. We can live without peanut butter or Special K or maple syrup. We pack in treats for one another from our home leaves—chocolate, good coffee. And if we were addicted to Blooming-dale's or Bergdorf's—well, then we probably wouldn't be here in the first place, would we?

No, what matters is the aloneness, an aloneness that extends to everything around us. During the Cultural Revolution the Party ordered the grass dug up, the wild birds hunted down and killed, and dogs and cats banned as pets. There are no colors or sounds or movements to distract us. Then there is the isolation. Shunning is a biblical punishment—isolate the sinners, ignore them, refuse them eye contact and conversation. The shunned call it torture. Here, an entire nation shuns us.

A request for directions on the street is met with a frightened stare and silence. Many of us are surreptitiously followed to see whom we meet. The few of us who have managed to make Chinese friends wrap ourselves in scarves and hats and venture out to prearranged locations only after dark. Much later, an embassy official will tell me that Beijing is far lonelier and more alienating than even her Peace Corps assignment was in an African village an hour's walk from the nearest town. Where she lived in Africa, she says, there was a gentle human contact that is almost totally missing in Beijing in 1984.

For centuries China has perfected the art of a formalized courtesy that keeps outsiders at bay. Casual visitors to Beijing come away charmed by the hospitality, the toasts, the speeches, the food. What few realize is that their second banquet will be identical to their first. And that the third and fourth will be the same as the opening two. And that the second month will have the identical scripted human contact as the first. The scripts are so well understood, and the fear of deviating from them so strong, that by my sixth month I can pass for fluent in Chinese. Anyone sitting next to me at a banquet would assume that I am a relaxed and confident conversationalist, when in reality I have simply memorized a dozen call-and-response tropes. How long have you been here? A year. Are you used to it? Oh yes, at first I was lonely, but now I am used to it. Do you like Chinese food? Yes, I do, I love Chinese food. China is a big country, with many people. Yes, indeed. That is true. China is very big. Do you have children? No, I don't. And you? A boy? Congratulations. A girl? Well, girls are good too.

When we leave our guarded compounds, we must walk fast, for otherwise a crowd will form. A silent, staring circle surrounds us whenever we pause. The bolder will reach out to touch. But mostly they just look. We feel like exotic beasts caged by curiosity in a very large zoo.

I respond to this by becoming smaller, retreating more and more into myself, curling inward into a small package. Terence is the opposite. He hurls his loneliness and frustration outward. He becomes as big as a volcano and every bit as unpredictable. Surrounded by a crowd on a particularly down day, I begin to cry. He, instead, takes a swing at the nearest gawker, a stopped cyclist, who saddles up and takes off in terror, pedaling as fast as he can go. At dinners and gatherings around town we routinely lament the conditions of our captivity. The rooms or apartments in which we are confined cost our employers fifty thousand dollars a year or more. There are two price tags for everything in China. One for the residents, another, ten times or more higher, for foreigners. Most of us grouse. Terence shouts.

"They are thieves! Lying, stealing thieves. All it is for them is gouge, gouge, gouge. How much can they gouge from the stupid foreigners? Lie! Lie! Lie! Gouge! Gouge! Gouge!"

He embarrasses and frightens me. I shout back.

"This is their culture. They are poor. We are rich. They just want to get as much as they can to improve their lives. You are such a bigot!"

"Since when is it bigoted to not like being gouged?" He gives no quarter. "They're thieves."

Others keep their complaints within the walls of diplomatic compounds and private conversations, smiling politely and toasting when outside. Not Terence. Every encounter is an opportunity for loud expression of his views.

When he decides that I cannot be a proper foreign correspondent without a trench coat he takes matters into his own hands. He brings a bolt of khaki material back to Beijing from one of his trips to the United States. He hustles me over to the Youyi Shangdian—the special Friendship Store where only foreigners are allowed to buy, and only with hard currency. Inside, a tiny tailor shop will make up clothes to order. He designs the Bogey-style coat himself, with a stand-up collar, a big leather buckle, and pockets for jamming my hands into. We are there for our first fitting. The model the tailor has produced is sloppily constructed and looks nothing like what Terence has drawn.

"You guys wonder why you're a third-world country? There's no excuse for this. Everything you do is half-assed and then you charge top dollar." His voice is crescendoing as he shouts down the woman behind the counter.

"What does this look like? What does this look like?" His Chinese is perfectly pitched.

She stands silent before the torrent.

"Does this look like what I gave you?" His face is red. His shouting is beginning to attract attention. I am embarrassed.

"I HATE YOU! I HATE ALL OF YOU!" he roars. "ALL OF YOU. I HATE YOU!"

WO HEN HEN NIMEN!

The guttural "h" and the sharply dropping fourth tone of the second *"hen"*—hate—make the outburst particularly effective.

I want to run. I want to hit him. I want to hide.

Somehow, however, everybody but me seems to figure Terence out.

A manager emerges from behind the curtain.

"What's going on?" he asks the clerk.

"He's mad at us again," she says.

"Oh," says the manager and turns back to his work.

Terence Bryan Foley.

Who is this strange man anyway?

Is he a spy?

His combination of nonstop revelation and a kind of hazy secrecy makes it very hard to answer that—or any other—question about him. I worry constantly that he is some kind of agent. For one thing, everyone I know thinks he is. For another, he will never answer the question consistently. Sometimes, he hoots with derision and mocks the questioners. "I'm a graduate of an Ivy League school. I was educated in New York," he says—Columbia University, it turns out. "I dress nicely and I speak fluent Chinese— none of your snobby East Coast journalist buddies can believe that I'm really from the Midwest and working for farmers. Soybeans? C'mon. Get REAL. The guy's GOTTA be a spy!"

Sometimes he simply sounds like the kind of moron who likes to tell half-truths to impress his girlfriend. "The CIA? Well, I'm not really *on the books . . .*"

Over the months I learn that he was born in 1940 in Cincinnati, Ohio, and was raised there, the fourth-generation son of a long line of German farmers and Irish immigrants. He had been trying to get to China all his life. Most improbably, he has been pursuing the romantic ideals of Song and Tang dynasty poets ever since he was a little boy. The pastor of the church Terence attended as a child had been raised in prerevolutionary China by his missionary parents. In 1952—the year I was born, in fact—he gave the twelve-year-old Terence a book of Chinese characters, and Terence was hooked. Terence began to study Chinese on his own, picking out the characters one by one. Later he enraged his par-

ents by dropping out of Ohio State University and, without telling them, enlisting in the navy, where he trained as a Chinese
language specialist. After he left the military, he finished his Chinese studies—picking up Japanese along the way—in New York.
Now he reads Li Po and Du Fu in the original, a feat much like a
Chinese speaker mastering Shakespeare and *Beowulf.*

His head is filled with plum blossoms and mists. He can recite
lines about the longing for a faraway home and about the conflicts
between honor and ambition. His mental China is made up of
shadowy scholars in long silken robes sitting under willow trees
steeping themselves in wine and poetic meter.

He has spent his entire adult life trying to reach this China of
his imagination, a place of delicacy and sophistication, erudition
and honor and dignity. The post-Mao China of squalor and spit-
ting and secrecy, poverty, public executions, venality, and suspi-
cion is almost more than his soul can bear. His fury at the Chinese
of today, it appears, stems at least partly from their failure to be
the Chinese of his imagination.

He is a fastidious dresser, in a style right out of *The Philadelphia
Story:* charcoal suits, often three-piece; bow ties, as I saw that first
day; felt hats; carefully polished black wingtips. He is disdainful
of anyone, including me, who is not careful about his or her ap-
pearance.

During the years when China was locked up tight to outsiders,
he worked with other countries. He spent years traveling around
the world, helping states market their dairy products and grains,
canned goods and fruits abroad. Then Terence saw his break
when Nixon visited China in 1972. Terence immediately sensed
that China was about to open to the West and shrewdly guessed
that agriculture would be the first field to begin to develop. He
began his preparations on the spot. He taught himself swine nutrition and poultry feed formulation and the Chinese vocabulary

to go along with it. He knew that China would want to learn modern agricultural techniques and that America would want to sell its products. He looked around for the most likely candidate and found it in soybeans. China was a huge consumer of soybeans; America a huge producer. With nothing more than his self-education and self-confidence, he wormed his way into a job with the American Soybean Association. U.S. soybean producers, he figured, would be among the earliest groups into China. He was right. In 1980, he became one of only a handful of foreigners allowed to live in Beijing as he opened the association's office.

When he talks about his work for the association, he is dead serious. He visits farms. He talks with farmers. He finds American experts at extension schools and brings them to China to teach the Chinese how to use soybeans to fatten their pigs, raise more chickens, farm fish, bottle soymilk.

Yet still I worry that all this is a cover for something darker. The worst times come when he senses I really need to know. Sometimes I grow nearly frantic. "Terence, I'm a journalist. If I'm hanging around with a spy, I could be in big trouble. You have to tell me..."

"I can't talk about that," he says, with an exaggerated deadpan air of mystery.

Eventually I conclude he is simply trying to annoy me.

One night at a fancy party at the British embassy, he wins a raffle. As he walks up to collect his prize, a free weekend in Hong Kong, some unknown voice behind me shouts: "Spook!" It sets my rage off anew. When he returns to the table full of plans for our newly acquired upcoming vacation, I refuse to speak to him.

We fight constantly. We fight from the moment we meet. We fight over meals. We fight in the car. We fight in the shower. We fight in bed. We trail each other down the street, each of us desperate to lose the other but more desperate not to lose the argument. We are blunt. We are not kind.

"You're not going out looking like that," he says. "You look like a bag lady." Me: "Only dorks wear bow ties." He thinks a friend who goes to work for a tobacco company must be banned from our lives; I think expressing disapproval is sufficient. I think my acquaintances are catholic and eclectic. He thinks I consort too readily with jerks. Edna St. Vincent Millay is a feminist genius. "She's a castrating bitch," he says. I think he gets worked up over nothing. He thinks journalists believe in nothing. I mock his speech—fireplug (It's a hydrant!). UM-brella. He mocks mine—coo-pon (Everyone knows it's kyoo-pon!). Roooo-f instead of ruh-f.

At Thanksgiving, I pull out a precious yellow cardboard box of Bell's Seasoning. I am pleased with myself. I have had the forethought to pack it with my incoming supplies. The smell of the ground thyme and sage, and the early morning toasting of the bread for stuffing is, for me, Thanksgiving and Christmas and home. We are going to stuff a scrawny chicken and pretend it is a turkey.

"You're not putting that chemical shit in my bird," he says.

MY bird? MY bird? Since when is it HIS bird? He has insulted me and attacked my childhood traditions. I, it turns out, have assaulted his sense of elegance. Stuffing is called "dressing" and it is created in a different manner every year. Prunes. Apricots (which he pronounces AY-pricots, not the proper AH-pricots). Almonds. Oysters. Ground sausage, or simmered giblets. And by the way, while it's proper to eat turkey at Thanksgiving—that's traditional—NO ONE eats turkey at Christmas. The correct Christmas meal is either a goose or roast beef and Yorkshire pudding. Bell's Seasoning plays no role in any of these holiday imaginings.

"We're not using this garbage," he says.

I snatch up the box, throw it at his head, and stomp out. I spend the next hour smoking and sulking on the street, while the usual curious crowd forms around me.

In truth, the reality of life in China has everyone on edge. For journalists every interview is a tedious ballet staged in meeting rooms with dozens of people arrayed in fat armchairs pushed back against the walls. Paying every bill takes an hour or more, carrying a wad of cash to a crowded office, standing in one line to pay, one to get a ticket for having paid, and back to the original line for the actual receipt. Phone connections are distant and tinny and cut off abruptly more often than they work.

The soybean association that Terence is working for is a government contractor that must meticulously account for every second of the day and every penny spent; I am working for a woman of temperament and ambition in whose eyes I can seemingly do nothing right. Yet she herself knows little about China and often makes absurd demands in the middle of the night. Her ignorance and impetuousness infuriate Terence. He rails on my behalf at stupid bosses all over the world.

He scares me with the way he talks to his own boss back home in the United States. I overhear him shouting into the phone across a 6,800-mile divide.

"No, I will NOT."

Silence.

"You will not do any such thing."

Silence.

"Goddammit. This is MY office, not yours."

He slams down the phone.

I am aghast. You are rude, reckless, undiplomatic, I say. You are spineless, he says. We fight about bosses. We fight about shouting. We fight about fighting.

We fight about jealousy. Just weeks before coming to China—
about eight months before I met Terence—I divorced the man I
had been with since I was nineteen years old. Before Terence and
I met, I was alone in China, halfway around the world, unmoored,
more emotionally strafed than I had expected or had the resources to deal with. Far from home, I had already flung myself
into destructive, blindingly wrong, inappropriate relationships
that had torn me up inside, and whose lingering traces were snak-
ing through our lives.

This is my problem, I say, not yours. You're killing me, he says.
This is none of your business, I say. It's nothing BUT my business.
But I am NOT marrying you. In any case, you're still married
yourself. Aha! Trump card! For that is one of the minor biographical details that has recently emerged. Terence is not yet divorced.
That's done, he says. Done. We've split up. In fact, he has been
living here alone in China since 1980, never even asking his wife
to visit. It is now 1984. In his view, he has been a single man for
nearly four years now. She's still your wife, I say.

Every little thing cuts one or the other of us like a razor. Two
wineglasses on a sink. An unanswered phone at midnight. A
dropped voice. A stray photograph. An unexplained postmark.
Ordinary actions—whether badly understood, misunderstood, or
understood only too clearly—become sanity-threatening betray-
als. Our emotions are toxic. Powerful. Colliding. I have never met
anyone before who can cause me so much pain. It will be a decade
before I fully realize that the same can be said for my effect on
him.

I do my job. I live on a farm to see the effects of Deng Xiao-
ping's agricultural reforms. I visit factories. Bathhouses. Peking
opera. President Reagan comes to visit. So does Nixon.

Terence does his job. The goal of the American Soybean Association is, of course, to get the Chinese to buy more soybeans
from American farmers. Terence's goal is nothing of the sort. He

has nothing but contempt for the *businessmen* (he says it like one would say "terrorist" or "prostitute") who want to *profit* from an underfed country. "I want to feed hungry people," he says.

There are hundreds of millions of hungry people in China. Even in the relatively well-nourished city, men are so thin their belts loop all the way around their narrow bodies and flap out the back. Workmen fall asleep on every possible surface. Cinder blocks. Piles of metal shavings. Few are getting entirely enough to eat, and certainly not enough protein. Terence thinks soy can change all that. Pigs are fed on table scraps, so he sets up pilot programs, raising sets of scrawny piglets on the traditional diet side by side with soy-fed animals that grow big and robust. He brings in new varieties of swine, bred for protein and away from fat. He brings in experts on chickens and eggs. He knows the proper composition of a chicken's diet in winter, and the proper composition in summer. He knows how to say "artificial insemination" and "ribonucleic acid" in Chinese. He travels to the south to teach aquaculture. To the north to help create bean curd plants. To the west to consider cattle.

Back in Beijing, his apartment is always full of strays. American students live in Chinese dorms, cold, with communal showers and toilets and little entertainment. I never know who I am going to find curled up in front of a movie eating his treats, or stepping out of the shower. On the street, he stops strangers, asking the proper pronunciation of odd words, trying out phrases on them. His American extension school experts are fond of down-home expressions. Terence is constantly looking for ways to translate. "He hit it out of the park." "He's a stand-up guy."

He pursues strange hobbies. One day I see him leave his room with a net, a jar, and a bizarre contraption with a mouthpiece and a double set of tubes.

"What are you doing?" I ask.

"I'm collecting bugs. Nobody has sent insect samples from

China to the Smithsonian for decades." He walks up to some
bushes beside the hotel, points the funnel-shaped cone at the
end of one tube at an unwary insect, and sucks sharply on the
other tube. Bernoulli's principle creates a swirling vacuum that
whooshes the bug into the jar in the middle. When he has several
samples, he preserves them and ships them off. "Terence is off
sucking bugs," I tell our friends.

He makes me order evening gowns tailored at the Friendship
Store, one a shimmering burgundy full-skirted silk, another an
aquamarine fitted sheath with spaghetti straps.

"Put on the burgundy dress," he says one evening. "We're going
out."

He arrives at my apartment dressed in full white tie. A black
tailcoat. White cummerbund and patent leather shoes. A cane
with an engraved silver knob. A top hat. He takes my arm. A Japanese restaurant has just opened in an old courtyard house. We sit
at the bar eating sushi and drinking beer. Then, looking just like
Fred Astaire, he leads me regally past the other gaping diners, my
silk dress sweeping the floor.

He woos me with rabbits and song.

I don't remember how the business about the bunnies began.
Maybe as an offhanded, sarcastic "none of your business" kind of
comment. In any case, it becomes a truism between us that the
reason my first husband, Philip, and I divorced was that I wanted
a rabbit and he would never get me one. It becomes a mindless,
repetitive joke that I mouth every time—and it is often—he
speaks of marriage.

"When are we going to get married?"

"You haven't given me my rabbit yet. After what I've been
through how can I marry another man who won't give me a
bunny?"

It feels particularly cold that December 1984. In Beijing in winter the wind whips down from Mongolia like a spear, bringing

with it the red dust of the Gobi Desert. When the wind blows you can't see across the street. Cyclists don face masks. The office furniture grows a grainy patina of desert sand and coal dust that must be wiped twice a day. Outside it is freezing. Inside, the office is overheated. I have my office door half closed, trying desperately to hear a telephone call through the static. I hear a commotion in the hall. I rise up, intending to close the door fully, when it flings open. Terence is wearing a green People's Liberation Army coat with the typical fake fur collar. The army hat with earflaps is pulled down low over his forehead. A scarf hides most of his face. He is carrying a cardboard box. He drops the box on my desk and stomps out.

Inside is not one bunny, but two. The little creatures are no bigger than my fist, with tiny ears the size of my pinkies. I can tell they are white, but just barely, through the thick orange dust that cakes them. Terence has spent the morning riding his bicycle, his own top-of-the-line Flying Pigeon, through freezing Beijing, crisscrossing the narrow *hutongs*, stopping to shout into the courtyards: Anyone in here raise rabbits? The bunnies move to the enclosed patio outside my office, where they grow fat on vegetable scraps and soybeans.

His work takes him away for long periods of time. He returns to the United States every other month, driving teams of Chinese farmers across the United States, observing U.S. farms, eating with American farmers, listening to translated lectures on essential minerals. While he is gone, I often receive strange letters. One is from a salesman of Chinese herbal medicine, promising me relief from headaches, bad skin, and "lady monthly cramp" if I only buy his brew of snake and dog penis. Another is from an eight-year-old, so excited about her first visit to China that she is sitting on the plane using pencils to practice eating with chopsticks.

Yet another day, I am sitting in my office when Miss Wang, my interpreter, comes in, a frightened look on her face.

"Amanda, does someone wish you harm?"

That morning a letter came in, written entirely in a beautiful Chinese script. I can't read Chinese, so I passed it on to her. As is. her habit, she produces a neat translation on lined paper.

Oh! My friends!
My friends who live in the city alongside the River!
There is big trouble coming your way!
Yes, I assure you, trouble is on its way to this city.
It is the ball game.
The ball game will bring you this trouble!

I read the message slowly, myself totally puzzled. Then I burst out laughing. The city alongside the river? River City! There's trouble in River City! Terence had translated Harold Hill's song from *The Music Man* into Chinese and mailed it to me from the road.

His trips also rip both of us in two. There is no easy phone contact back to the United States—calls must be booked far ahead, sometimes as much as twenty-four hours in advance. He's seldom in one location long enough for us to talk. Since we fight constantly, every trip is an opportunity for two weeks of unresolved misery. After one fight, he flees my apartment. Furious, I wait till the following day, the eve of his departure, to call. No answer. Ten minutes later. No answer. No answer. No answer. No answer. I run the ten blocks to the Jianguo and find him madly packing, the phone pulled out of the wall.

I am unhappy when he is around. I am miserable when he is gone. I drive him to the airport and sit in the parking lot watching him go. I cry and cry and cry. How will I survive Beijing for the next ten days? The last day is the hardest. If I can make it to bedtime, then I can sleep. When I wake up in the morning, I can leave right away for the airport. He will be in at eleven. The phone rings at midnight. "I've missed my plane," in San Francisco. It will be twenty-four hours till the next one. How will I fill the hours till then? Time crawls. Work weighs heavy. The hours between dark and dawn are leaden. Sometimes I awaken suddenly at 2:00 or 3:00 a.m. When he is gone, I am alone, and the black night is mine to fill with nothing.

Do I love him? Do I hate him? I can barely tell the difference. I do know that I need him, and I'm pretty sure I don't like that fact at all. On his forty-fifth birthday in 1985 I don the burgundy silk dress again, low cut and shimmering. "Put on your tux," I command. "Meet me at this corner." I name an intersection at the very edge of the area where foreigners are allowed to visit.

At 5:00 p.m., I go to fetch him there and find him standing at the dusty crossroads in the September chill. Bicycles zip past him. Peasants are sitting by the side of the road selling vegetables off spread-out blankets. Three-wheel motor carts, called *san lun che*, tootle past, filled with metal shavings, lengths of pipe, pyramids of cabbages, bolts of burlap. Terence's tuxedo pants are nicely creased, his shoes perfectly polished.

We are just outside the Summer Palace, the country retreat that the Empress Dowager Cixi starved the Chinese navy of its silver to perfect. In September, the palace's Kunming Lake is slate flat and clear, reflecting Longevity Hill on its surface. There is nothing that looks more like the China of Terence's dreams than the Summer Palace. Stacked pagodas with their rounded tops are tucked into the elbows of the surrounding hills. Branches curve delicately down to the water. As night falls, a light fog hovers on the lake's surface.

My time in China is growing short. It is early September. I will

leave here for good just before Thanksgiving. Tonight, I have
rented an old barge and a bargeman for us alone. Earlier that afternoon, I scoured Beijing for every treat I could find. I bought
French bread and salami from the Jianguo Hotel. At the Friendship Store, I grabbed some big tubs of the four-dollar caviar that
the Russians love. I liberated some cornichons and olives from my
shipped-in stash.

The boatman putt-putts into the center of the lake and cuts the
engine. The sun is setting. We are in a Chinese painting. The light
fog tickles the arched bridges over the footpaths. I have a shawl,
but I am still chilly. Terence throws his tuxedo jacket over my
shoulders. I have borrowed a tape player from a neighbor; "Ten-
nessee Waltz" and "Unchained Melody" are playing in the background. We drink Great Wall white wine, a new Chinese variety
that tastes something like a cross between Riesling and Kool-Aid.
We dance on the barge's flat deck.

As darkness falls and the stars come out, I am thinking: This
will be a pleasant last memory for us both. Thank God I am leaving before he drives me completely insane.

2

Later I wonder: Should we have seen it coming? Perhaps we should have seen that it was in his genes all along. But when the death of his mother from cancer brings Terence and me back together again in Florida on Thursday, March 13, 1986, he and I are both very much alive and glad to be so. We are not thinking of our own mortality.

We are flying.

The Cessna skirts the Florida coast then banks, turns, and heads back to the landing strip. Terence is at the controls, an instructor beside him. I am in the back. He gently guides the plane down, lets the tires barely touch the ground, and accelerates back up into the air. Over and over he does that. Bank, turn, touch, rise. I look out over the ocean, nearly still, the waves marked only by thin white ripples.

It is March 1986. Back home in New York, where I now live, it is still winter, the sky muddy and gray. Here in Florida it is a glorious sapphire spring, verging on summer already, warm and clear.

The instructor hands Terence a helmet. He straps it on and he can no longer see the sky, the sea, or the narrow swath of ground where he is to land, only the controls. Now he is flying blind.

It has been more than four months since we last saw each other in Beijing. My Thanksgiving 1985 departure from China did not end our relationship as I expected, and perhaps even had half hoped. I moved to New York, still with *The Wall Street Journal*. He stayed on in Beijing, a year more to fulfill on his contract. Yet even

6,800 miles, life on the opposite sides of day and night, five-dollar-a-minute phone charges, and our still-constant fighting don't succeed in prying us apart. We spend hundreds of dollars on calls. We talk. We fight. We make up. When I leave my Manhattan studio, even for a short errand, I am always in agony lest he call while I am gone. I finally buy myself some psychic freedom in the form of an answering machine. When I see the red blinking light and hear the operator's nasal Chinese, *"Mei you ren jie"*—No one is answering—at least I know he is reaching out.

While I live in New York, he is still in China visiting farms and factories, promoting American soybeans. For the last few weeks, though, he has been in Cincinnati sitting at his mother's side in a nursing home as her cancer slowly kills her. When he calls me, I can hear her in the background. She is screaming. She is in pain. He buys her grapes, and raspberries, and the two of them inch their way toward the conversations they were unable to have when she was well.

He had cancer himself many years ago, when he was still almost a boy. He was shaving at home on one of his leaves from the navy when his mother spotted an ugly bluish patch on his shoulder. By the time Terence and I met, the only souvenir of that episode was a scar that looked like a map of Texas. She caught it early before it metastasized, he told me, leaving him with nothing worse than a sore shoulder.

Ruth, his mother, isn't so lucky. Though she and Terence were estranged for years, she suddenly called him in China. Come home at once, she said. I am dying. I never got to meet her. He has just buried her and must return to China on Monday. Her illness and death have seemed to energize Terence with a frantic, almost manic, life. Perhaps her illness—and Terence's own youthful bout with melanoma—should have alerted us that something was lurking in the background. It did not.

We meet in Florida to give him a break before he heads back to

Beijing. This trip is supposed to afford him some rest. I fly down from Manhattan to join him.

Our reunion is visceral, not romantic or tender. Once again we collide with the inevitability of thunder. He is not resting. He is not sentimental. He isn't mourning his mother, or at least he doesn't seem to be. He is barely sitting still. He is on fire. Is he glad to see me? I can't tell. Am I glad to see him? I'm not sure. All I know is that we need to be together.

He has two plans for this weekend. He is already a licensed pilot. He tells me about a time when, flying alone in just such perfect weather, he was swallowed up by a sudden and unexpected storm. He flew lost and frightened for at least fifteen minutes completely enveloped in fog and rain, unable to tell east from west or even, at times, up from down. He never wants to do that again. He is going to learn to fly by instruments, and he is going to do it NOW. Not only that, while he is here he is also going to become a helicopter pilot. A contact here has offered him some helicopter time in exchange for business leads in China. He is determined to get both licenses before he leaves.

That night, Terence sits with a four-inch binder on his knees. He is switching back and forth between the rules for planes and those for helicopters.

"I've got to book it. Hard," he says, barely stopping for a quick dinner. "I may have to go all night." There are hundreds of pages of rules, instructions, technical terms to learn in order to pass a written and an oral exam with a Federal Aviation Administration instructor. He is frantically taking notes. What's more, he's going to need at least forty hours of helicopter flight time. Most people take a year or more to get each license.

He's going to do it in four days.

"That can't be done!" I protest. Why can he not see that? Four days equals only ninety-six hours. It won't work.

His face clouds. He sees something entirely different. Ten

hours of flight time a day for four days equals forty hours. That leaves fifty-six hours for study and the exam. He and I have already spent two hours in the Cessna and, before I arrived, he spent two hours with an instructor mastering the controls of a Robinson R22 helicopter. It's tricky, he says, more three-dimensional than the fixed-wing planes he is used to flying. But it's not impossible.

Not impossible? It's lunacy!

"You're undermining my self-confidence." He's shouting. This isn't a joke or a game. Nothing about this is funny to him, or odd. "If I'm going to do this, I need to stay focused." I am bewildered. Angry that he is ignoring me. Frightened at his intensity, his obsession. I realize once again that we don't just see the world differently. In many ways we don't live in the same world at all. He is going to become a helicopter pilot in four days? Is the man truly mad? Am I mad for thinking about twining my life with his?

Just over a year later, on May 26, 1987, we are married at Christ and St. Stephen's Church on West Sixty-ninth Street in Manhattan. It is pouring rain.

Terence's soybean contract expired, he packed up his apartment in Beijing, and the two of us have now crammed our belongings into a tiny studio near Central Park.

At our wedding, we have: a red and white horse-drawn carriage. I have: a champagne-colored tea dress, an Ingrid Bergman hat, and arms filled with peonies. He has: his buddy Sean, a Marine Corps colonel, standing up for him in his dress blues. My mother loses the rest of the group between the hotel and the church and must lace her way, street by street, in the downpour until she recognizes the church. Alone with Sean back in the nave, Terence knows none of this. All he knows is that he is hearing the trumpet player begin to improvise, and it is half past the hour.

"She has changed her mind," he says to Sean. "They're afraid to come back here and tell me." Yet my mother finds the church, the trumpet launches into a voluntary, the rain stops as suddenly as it began, the sun bursts out, and we are married.

In fact, by Chinese custom, if not law, we've been married for quite some time now. A Chinese legal marriage is a dull bureaucratic event—papers and chops in a government office. There is no tradition of church weddings. Even a house of one's own can be hard to get in Communist China. Many couples consider themselves actually "married" by their wedding photo. Just before I leave China, Terence insists that we have one taken.

We line up at the photo studio where a shop assistant is handing out what I can only think of as costumes. There are a dozen one-size-fits-all-dream-of-an-American-pouffe wedding gowns. Girls of all shapes wait to don them. We drop them over our street clothes, the dresser pins them in back and gathers up the train. We stand in line, twelve of us in a row, the bundled fabric in our arms. One at a time we step onto the set, a Greco-Italian *Gone with the Wind* painting with columns and a half-nude statue and painted red-carpeted steps rising up behind us. The dresser drops the train, swirls it around me, lifts the veil from the previous girl's head, and sets it on mine. He ignores Terence, whose own tailcoat and top hat are far grander than anything the studio can provide. The photographer snaps, we move out of the scene, and I turn the gown over to the next girl in line, who immediately dons it.

I mock the campy fun of the photo shoot. My flyaway hair in the photo speaks more of carelessness than elegance; the look on my colorized face in the photo is more smirk than dewy-eyed. Terence is all romance. We fight about that too.

After the dreary bleakness of Beijing, New York is a riot of color and sound and energy. Behind us, the Wall Street barbarians are already massing at the gate, but we don't know that yet. Right now all we can hear are the drums and the cymbals. The Street is a fun career for young people, and they are leaking money out into all the other streets of the city. The old groceries with faded linoleum floors are being displaced by stores with "Emporium" in their names and sushi bars inside. Korean vendors parade pyramids of fruit—oranges, pomegranates, dozens of varieties of apples—on nearly every corner. At work, technicians hand out clunky electronic boxes that we can actually use for writing stories. ATMs grow less likely to eat our plastic cards and quickly become reliable enough that we can begin to count on them for weekend money. Prosperity creeps out from Broadway. Warehoused buildings along Amsterdam Avenue and Columbus sprout bars, restaurants, and condos. Break dancers cavort on corners.

For all our fighting, we like being married. We settle into the one-room apartment around the corner from Lincoln Center. We run in Central Park. We see movies with subtitles. We climb all the way up to the top balcony at the Metropolitan Opera and watch *La Bohème* and *Rigoletto*. We linger on the traffic island between Broadway and Amsterdam to kiss and pat before parting. We laugh at the downstairs neighbor who complains about our footsteps above his head. At first we are sympathetic, until he explains we are disturbing his séances. Within a few months, our 452 square feet of space is as stuffed as his apartment in Beijing. Books. Notebooks. Trombones. Trumpets. He is a musician at heart, who can play any instrument invented. Tubas piled on our bed. Every night we must relocate them so we can sleep; every morning they go back on the bed so we can walk around the room.

By Christmas, I must walk sideways down the narrow entry corridor to the room where we actually live.

Yet neither the photo marriage nor the real one magically transforms us. To the contrary, the tighter we are bound together, it seems, the more we struggle against it. Our fights take on a

Manhattan feel. We court death nearly every day as, crossing the street, I list to the left and he to the right. Jamming into each other in the middle of the street and refusing to back down. Do we want the check now? Simultaneously: "Yes." "No." After I slam the door, I can mentally rehash our argument at a movie theater down the street or show up full of righteous ire at my friend Deb's door ten blocks away. When he storms away, he can wait it out at a jazz bar around the corner. We both have words at our command and powerful, unyielding personalities. From the safe distance of time, in our warm kitchen in Philadelphia, Terence's explanation of that era will be the mirror image of mine: "You were crazy back then," he says shaking his head. "A real nut case."

So why do we stay together?

I honestly don't know. I think we can't help ourselves. In addition, from the beginning I think we each have seen in the other the parent for the children we want to have. He is forty-seven. I am thirty-five. For reasons neither of us can explain, we both desperately want children—with each other. Yet even in this we clash. After a miscarriage, I am laid low by grief; he finds refuge in a manic cheer.

Yet, when Terence Bennett Foley is born on October 26, 1988, under a fat harvest moon, it is immediately clear that we are both very good parents. Terence sits up all night arranging movie marathons for me. *The Ghost and Mrs. Muir. White Heat.* A run of Edward G. Robinson: *Key Largo. Double Indemnity. Brother Orchid.* Feeding our son, I watch the movies. Terence watches us.

A father for the first time at age forty-eight, he radiates the belief that there has never been another such perfect child born into this world. He freely admits hostility to other people's offspring. He lives for discussion, for argument, for intellectual debate. Children, with their fingers and noses and whining and lap-climbing feints for attention, are the natural enemy of such adult discourse. Yet little Terry has but to chirp and conversation stops. Terence frets over Cheerios and apple juice, wraps Terry like a papoose against the smallest wind, takes note after note after note on his progress on the index cards that he keeps in his breast pocket.

Our friend Isabelle from Paris gives a Gallic shrug about her own such besottedness. "I felt so sor-REE for ze ozther mozthers who had such u-GLEE bay-BEES," she says. Terence smiles politely. She may have been mistaken. He is not.

Nothing our little boy touches can be thrown away. Years later, I have only to go over on any Saturday afternoon to the storage unit on an old pier on the Delaware River that divides Philadelphia from New Jersey and open the door to our twelve-foot-by-fifteen-foot unit to see the outcome. One whole wall of the unit is stacked floor to ceiling with boxes marked "Memorabilia." I open them and find the sedimentary layers of a family at its beginning. The quacking pull-string duck. Chime bird. A sailor suit. A train set. *Cars and Trucks and Things That Go.* A crayon scrawl.

When our daughter Georgia arrives nine years later her childhood layers begin. A green velvet dress with a lace collar. A pair of white gloves. *Brown Bear, Brown Bear.* A pressed rose bouquet. Everyone saves such things. Terence saves EVERYTHING. He throws himself at recording his children's lives with the same energy he pours into trying to pilot helicopters.

3

The late 1980s and early '90s are not easy years, and Manhattan is not an easy place, for a nearly fifty-year-old man to be looking for work. Not even six months after we marry comes Black Monday. The stock market crashes a breathtaking five hundred points and the Manhattan party comes to a screeching halt. There is probably never a good year for anyone with a lifetime in agriculture to be looking for work in Manhattan. He is offered a job in his field. In Pierre, South Dakota. We consider it. For a moment.

Meanwhile, the topic of my book, the downsizing of American corporations, is playing out in our living room. Terence's degree. His China connections. His lifetime of experience. His sheer dogged intellect. They all drive him close to nearly every job. But there at the top there is always someone better. Someone just perfect. Someone whose entire life has prepared him or her for just that job. He comes heartbreakingly close time after time after time.

He reinvents himself once, twice, three times. We recast his résumés. Agriculture. China. Marketing. Teaching. Food. He gets a job with an organization promoting China to business. He leaves it, unable to bear working side by side with people who know so much less than he does. He gets a job marketing gourmet food products to department stores. Long, exhausting days take their toll. He takes a class and learns to become a real estate appraiser. He goes into neighborhoods where it can be fatal to be simply standing on the wrong corner at the wrong time. He reassures me.

He has figured out the system. He makes appointments at 7:00 a.m. All the bad guys are sleeping it off by then, he says. Every day I hold my breath till he calls me, safely back in the office.

We send out letters by the dozens. Hundreds. If any answer comes back, it is disappointing. Underqualified. Overqualified. Not qualified at all. Out go more letters. Back come more answers. Or no answer at all.

One day I am getting lunch in the cafeteria at *The Wall Street Journal* when, much to my amazement, I spot him filling his tray.

"What are you doing here?" I ask. "Aren't you supposed to be at work?"

"I am," he says. "I work here."

My jaw drops.

Without telling me, he has reinvented himself yet again, this time as a radio journalist. A few months earlier, discouraged by yet another "unqualified" response, this time for a Hong Kong–based job, he dashes off a "résumé" and sends it back. "This qualified enough for you?" is his curt message to the rejecter. Of course he never hears back. Then, on a whim, he takes the same résumé and sends it to a few places just at random. At the *Journal* it lands on the desk of someone with a sense of humor and an eye for writing.

Here is the résumé he submits:

Terence Bryan Foley
235 West 102 Street #6-1
New York, New York 10025
H 212-222-2995
O 718-339-2500

Job Experience;

1988-1990. SECRETARY GENERAL OF THE UNITED NATIONS, NY, NY.
Preside over global disputes . Direct humanitarian
policy. Conduct meetings. Save the world.

1986-1988. SENATE MAJORITY LEADER, WASHINGTON. D.C.
Preside over partisan political activity. Formulate
political policy. Enforce discipline. Evade blame.

1984-1986. PRESIDENT, HARVARD UNIVERSITY, CAMBRIDGE, MASS.
Preside over major academic institution. Formulate
educational policy. Officiate at ceremonies.

1982-1984. COMMANDANT, U.S. MILITARY ACADEMY, WEST POINT, NY.
Preside over major military institution. Formulate
educational policy. Officiate at ceremonies.

1980-1982. CHIEF EXECUTIVE OFFICER, GENERAL MOTORS, DETROIT.
Preside over major heavy industry. Formulate industrial policy. Support protectionism. Blame Japan.

1978-1980. DIRECTOR, CENTRAL INTELLIGENCE AGENCY, LANGLEY, VA.
Preside over major intelligence facility. Formulate
intelligence policy. High-speed auto chases. Women.

1975-1978. PAPAL NUNCIO, VATICAN, ROME.
Preside over medieval religious domain. Formulate
theological policy. Officiate at ceremonies.
Awards;

Eagle Scout. Heissman Trophy Winner. Pulitzer Prize. Nobel
Peace Prize. Medal of Honor. Canonization. Webelos Badge.
Schneider Trophy. MVP. NYC Lottery Winner. Croix de Guerre.

Activities;

Astronaut. Saved tropical rain forests. Discovered pasteuriza-
tion, pi, Bernoulli's principle, penicillin. Invented perpetual
motion machine.

One of the many jobs in Terence's past was radio announcer. He has a beautiful, deep, resonant bass and a newsreel pronunciation. He is a fast, clever, witty writer. He gets the job. We work there together for months before anyone even realizes we are related.

Five years go by. I write one book, then another. We are still good parents—at opposite ends of the spectrum. I crawl on my belly like a snake, peeking around corners to make Terry laugh; Terence sits him on his knee and reads "Rumpelstiltskin." I plop a naked boy in the bath with tubs of finger paint and let him decorate himself and the walls; Terence creates artful Halloween costumes out of nothing. A Batman cape and mask. A Robin Hood, with a loden green doublet, a peaked cap, and a quiver, all sewn with a needle and thread. I buy OshKosh and corduroys and sneakers. Terence dresses him like Little Lord Fauntleroy, in sailor suits, short pants and knee socks, polished shoes and clip-on bow ties. I make us go camping. He makes us go to church. I cook wild stir-fries and curries. He makes us sit down every night to eat them. We hold hands. We say grace.

"Your idea of a family is like a 1950s cigarette ad," I complain. Dad in a tie, with the paper. Me in a housedress, with knitting. The little boy in short pants on the braided rug, running his toy cars up and down as the news comes over the radio.

"You were raised by savages," he says.

He fills the house with Christmas. Every person we have ever met is invited. We move our furniture into the hall. Guests cram so tightly in that they are forced to make conversation with strangers. Terence cooks and bakes. Lasagna. Christmas cookies. Chili. Pumpkin bread. Spice cake. He feeds two hundred people and has leftovers. The smell of mulled wine curls through with the scent of cinnamon and cloves. One Christmas week bad weather strands me in Los Angeles, unable to make it home for the party. Guests arrive, ask after me. "She's in the bathroom," Terence tells each one. Hours go by. "Is she sick?" they ask.

We go to marriage counseling. We trip over each other's voices trying to explain our conflicts. The counselor speaks in a soothing professional voice and suggests an exercise. Why don't we go home, sit down in the middle of the living room floor, and take turns giving each other back rubs, as a way of building trust—

We simultaneously explode in indignation.

"I read that in *Ladies' Home Journal*," I say, accusingly.

"Buddy, touching each other is not one of our problems," says Terence.

Out on the sidewalk, we storm wordlessly side by side. A thought suddenly occurs to me. Perhaps I am making HIM as miserable as he is making ME. It is the first time this thought has occurred to me. I reach for his hand. He takes it.

4

We find the cancer by accident, on Sunday, November 5, 2000, in the emergency room of Providence St. Vincent Medical Center in Portland, Oregon. We don't recognize it when we see it. We are looking for something else when we find it, the source of a long-standing pain in Terence's gut. When the doctors point out the cancer we try to ignore them. We consider it a nuisance. A distraction from what we think is the real illness that has been bedeviling him.

We live in Portland now, having arrived here from New York via Atlanta. Terence was born for adventure. When we walk the streets of New York, he points up at bay windows. "I want to live there," he says. After dinner in Chinatown, he points up at an apartment above the teeming streets. "Let's move there."

So when, after nearly a decade in New York, the *Journal* offers in 1995 to make me a manager in Atlanta, I hesitate. He does not. I have always been a reporter, in charge of no one but myself. Now that will change. It scares me.

"You're going to be somebody, Toots," he says. "I've told you that all along."

He is ready to go long before I am.

"My idea of fun," he says, "is moving to a different place every year. I love new places. I love learning new things. I love meeting new people." So off we go, and I become not just bossy but a boss, for the first time in my life.

In New York, Terence stands out for his dignified, Midwestern formality. In Atlanta, for his bohemian eccentricity. In our new suburban world of cul-de-sacs and swimming pools and center-hall colonials, regional sales managers, silver Lexuses and black SUVs, he buys a twenty-year-old Volvo, with two hundred thousand miles on it. One morning the entire front crashes to the ground, stopping traffic in both directions for fifteen minutes. Our neighbors hire gardeners to edge their front lawns. Terence plants pumpkins and sunflowers in ours; had I not become hysterical, he would have planted corn.

I fret that I am not like the other women, who have embroidered sweaters for every season, nice hair and nails and tidy homes. He is smug that he is not like the other men. At brunch, I watch from the kitchen as Terence and a tall man in khakis and a polo shirt—a district manager for some company making some thing—sit side by side in the family room.

"Play much golf?" our neighbor asks.

"No," says Terence.

They finger their drinks in silence. If the man is stupid enough not to recognize the importance of Sarajevo, or of Atget and Margaret Bourke-White, or Bix Beiderbecke, or the problems of translating four-character Chinese sayings into English... well, Terence can't help him.

Terence goes to work at CNN, creating historical and political context for news stories online. He rails at his twenty-eight-year-old colleagues who can't tell a flattop from a battleship, or who can't place Turkey on a map—and don't seem to care. Our own small neighborhood is filled with children. Evan. Michael. Tessa. Leah. Louis. Lawton. Terence throws himself into coaching at the Baptist church down the street. I join them after work, my heels sinking in the soft earth. He sends away for official coaching manuals. He and Terry do endless grounders and pop-ups in the front yard.

Our new home is three times bigger than anything we have lived in before—four bedrooms, a two-car garage, a finished basement, and a storage area. He fills them all. Before the year is out we cannot use the garage for a garage. We cannot use the basement for a playroom. We cannot use the laundry room for laundry without lifting stacks of newspapers waiting to be clipped off the tops of the machines. One day I slip and the whole edifice collapses, instantly forming papier-mâché with laundry water and detergent. I lie down on the kitchen floor and begin to cry. "I can't take it. I can't take it," I sob over and over again. He is frightened. The papers are gone by morning.

The Olympics come and go. A backpack bomber kills a bystander; a security guard is falsely charged. The Unabomber is arrested and Dolly the sheep is cloned. Yet by Terry's eighth birthday we still do not have the little girl we want. We turn back to China, where the one-child policy is swelling orphanages around the country with girls—perfect in every way, except for their sex. We write essays. Get recommendations. Ink our fingers at the local police station. A social worker visits our home to check us for suitability.

More than a year later, in January of 1998, the fax arrives in the middle of the night with a thumbnail photo of a sad-eyed child with a ragged haircut. Terry, Terence, and I set off for China in February 1998 to pick up little Liu Yue, who will be renamed Georgia Anne Bennett Foley.

She is nearly four years old, a southern girl, from Wuhan, China's equivalent of Atlanta. It is immediately clear to Terence and me that, a little more than a decade since we left, the China that we knew is fading into the past, and a new, glittery China is emerging. Wuhan is a midsize city of 7.6 million. There are cars on the street. Lots of cars. We stock up our hotel room with juice boxes and cartons of milk that we buy at the supermarket. There is even a shiny new department store downtown. Georgia's Chinese is fluent, if heavily accented. Terence and I want her to keep her language, so we speak to her only in Chinese.

She has other ideas. Barely two weeks after she comes home, she flies around Terry's Little League practice with the other kids.

"Frenchyfry shlushy. Frenchyfry shlushy," she chants. It gets her the junk food she wants. Terence stubbornly continues to speak to her in Chinese, but she just as stubbornly puts her hands over her ears and refuses to listen.

By June 1998, I have been with *The Wall Street Journal* for twenty-three years. I am forty-six years old, and I am being offered an excellent job in Oregon by Sandra Rowe, a woman I admire, and will come to love. Yet again I am afraid. His answer to all my objections is the same. "You are going to be somebody, Toots. It's about time you started." I close my eyes and jump.

The plan is for me to go on ahead. Terence will stay behind to close up the house. When school ends, Terry and Georgia will fly to Oregon with Anja, their longtime babysitter. They are nervous. Terry has never flown without us; Georgia has been on a plane only once in her life. Terence hits on an idea. "Give them something to take care of," he says. "It will help them forget about themselves." We buy a taffy-colored gerbil and a small traveling case. Caramel has never flown before, Terence tells them. They must help him be brave. Off they go, across the country, carefully tending the gerbil through boarding, landing, a plane change. As soon as they arrive, and I meet them at the plane, our first call is to Daddy, to let him know that Caramel has landed and is going to be very happy in his new home.

And for two and a half years, we are.

· · ·

By the time the emergency room doctors discover the cancer, Terence and I have been married for more than thirteen years. Georgia is now six, and Terry has just turned twelve. Our family has a life together in Oregon.

With the discovery of the cancer, you might suppose we feel: This is where our whole life changes. This is where everything becomes different. But it isn't like that at all. As soon as we discover it, it becomes an afterthought, a nuisance, a distraction from another more demanding illness and everything else going on in our lives. The doctors call it a "shadow."

On the morning of our discovery, the house is filled with not-quite-adolescent boys, celebrating Terry's twelfth birthday. We'd let them set up a tent in the family room the night before, stowed everything breakable, given them all pillows and flashlights, and let them romp through the house. Terence hadn't been feeling well for several weeks. Still, he is pummeling boys with pillows and fending off their attacks as he videotapes the mayhem. By 11:00 a.m. I am rousting bleary-eyed boys, filling them with pancakes, and shipping them home one by one as parents arrive. Terence is nowhere to be found.

I find him on our bed doubled over in pain. I'm scared. He's trying not to moan. I call our family doctor, who orders us to the emergency room right away. When the last boy is picked up, I bundle Terence and the two kids into the car and head across town. We pack bags of toys for both children, preparing for a long wait at the emergency room.

Instead, when the triage nurse takes his name, age, and symptoms, Terence is whisked past the waiting room filled with other patients right into a curtained alcove. That alarms me even more.

What do they know that we don't? Not wanting to frighten the children, Terence has clenched his jaw all the way to the hospital, but once the kids are installed out in the cheerful large outer waiting area with their X-Men and Barbies, the pain breaks through. On the emergency gurney, he curls into a fetal position and keens in pain. He is wheeled off for a scan almost immediately.

After reading the scan, the attending doctor is vaguely reassuring. Something is clearly wrong with his intestines, but there doesn't appear to be any immediate danger. Almost as an aside, however, he mentions that on the scan a "shadow" has appeared on Terence's kidney. "You are going to want to get that looked at," he says in a very casual tone.

Terence and I are both annoyed. Why is he even talking about a shadow? Who cares about a shadow? His kidneys aren't the problem. It's his intestines. He is in such pain from his gut he can scarcely breathe. He is admitted to the hospital directly from the emergency room with a diagnosis of severe ulcerative colitis.

Pain.

It is the thing I recall most clearly from the next five weeks. Terence in pain. He is white with pain, curled up from pain, almost completely consumed with pain. No food. No water. Nothing by mouth, says the chart on his bed. They pump him full of steroids to reduce the inflammation in his colon. Every morning I come by hoping to catch a doctor; every evening I bring the children by with a handmade card, or one of their toys. The children and I eat dinner in the hospital every night. Chili. Meatloaf. Grilled chicken from the cafeteria. Terry plays Christmas carols on a grand piano in the dining room. Georgia learns to work the soft-ice-cream machine. Upstairs, Terence lies half-crazed with the pain. He loses sixty pounds.

Six days later, he is sent home, still in pain, but at least able to stand upright. Let's see if the severity of the attack subsides, they say. It's the best we can do. Terence forces himself back to work; I drop him on the corner right outside the door of Portland State, where he is teaching a class on imperialism. When we drive, he cries out at every turn, almost shrieking at potholes. The pain is just barely to the side of endurable.

Just barely.

After several weeks of this, he is in bed one night, his teeth clenched from the agony in his gut. He starts a conversation with me that begins in the middle.

"I won't leave a mess for you or the children to find," he says. He gives me no room to answer. He is planning. "I can't take this much longer," he says. "I'll go out into the woods. I'll leave directions so you can send someone." I know he has guns, locked somewhere safely away from the children—and from me. I don't know where they are or how to find them.

The steroids aren't working. Withholding food isn't working. Time isn't healing. All along there has been another choice, a drastic one. Now it is clear it is time to make it. On December 13, 2000, Dr. David Luallin removes Terence's entire colon.

Emerging from the operation, Dr. Luallin has two things to say. The first is that the operation has been successful. The colon— damaged mysteriously beyond any help, he says—is gone now, and with it the pain. Terence will face several more operations to restore his digestive functions, but there will be no more pain. Second, there is definitely something on the kidney. He saw it while he was inside. A "cyst" he calls it. Of those two sentences, I ignore one, focusing instead on the other, thanking God we ended Terence's pain before he was tempted again to do so himself.

Of all the things we fight about, the big three of most couples' contention—sex, money, and child rearing—play no role in our lives. On all three we seem to have a deep, visceral alignment. We arrive at our view of money from different poles. He grew up with plenty of it; my childhood was always panicked lest there not be enough. Somehow we have arrived at the same utilitarian view of it. We think about it like we think about plumbing. It's got to be there. It's got to work. Otherwise, we ignore it. I often ignore it to the point of chaos. It's never unusual to find me paying the same bill twice, or three times, or not at all. I set up systems and promptly ignore them. I get overwhelmed by details and paper. Every couple of months, Terence sits me down and slowly works with me to unravel the latest disaster I have created.

So I pay no attention whatsoever to the cost of the surgery. I'm not even sure who is paying for it. Because I have a good job, I have good health insurance courtesy of my employer, *The Oregonian*. In this I am typical—one of the more than 80 percent of Americans covered by either private or government insurance. Still, I confess to being a bit hazy about who is actually paying the bills. The sheets of paper we get every time we go to a doctor say "Blue Cross/Blue Shield," so in some vague way I think it's "insurance" covering the cost, even though I will come to learn that it is really my employer paying all along. Blue Cross just handles the details.

We had just had an example of how a minor slip-up in that system could cost us a lot. Georgia, who had arrived in our family from China with a mouthful of rotten baby teeth, is so terrified of the dentist that he can't keep her still long enough even to give her anesthetic. Terence calls me at work: The dentist wants to run her over to the local community hospital, where he can put her under for the few minutes it will take to pull the teeth. A few weeks later, we receive a $1,500 bill for the dentist's fifteen-minute use of the operating room. The hospital has no agreement with the insurance company. The bill is ours.

When it comes to Terence's colon surgery, Dr. Campbell, the soft-spoken family doctor who practices out of a modest strip mall, has obviously had experience with this insurance situation. When he orders us to the emergency room, he says, almost as an aside, "Be sure to go to one of the Providence Hospitals, They'll take your insurance." A patient he had just sent by ambulance to the nearest hospital is now facing tens of thousands of dollars of un-covered bills. That patient happened to have the same insurance coverage as we do, he explains—Regence Blue Cross Blue Shield of Oregon—so Dr. Campbell remembers what to tell us to do.

I also wonder if I would have been so careless had I seen the actual bills. I'm sure they came to the house after Terence's hospi-talization. I paid what little part was our share and threw away the rest. The bills for the first stay totaled $10,595, including $661 a day for the bed. For the second stay, which includes the hours-long surgery, the hospital bills totaled $44,626.32; the surgeon, Dr. David Luallin, billed $3,503; and the anesthesiologists $1,595.

That Christmas, in the year 2000, the children and I buy the big-gest, bushiest, fattest Christmas tree that the Oregon forest can give us. Terry and Georgia and I drive out to a farm in the wispy Oregon mist to pick it out. The children select a huge Douglas fir. I think it cost about seventy-five dollars, which is way more ex-pensive than the ones Terence and I usually would buy. Yet it is tall and perfectly conical with lush full needles and the smell of the woods still on it. It is so big that the three of us can't handle it ourselves. Sandy, my boss, sends her husband and a friend over to set it up and help us string lights.

We move the piano and set the tree up in a corner of the living room, where two banks of windows meet, looking straight down at the Willamette River. It is an offering of sorts.

Back when we were moving here more than two years ago, Terence and I fought over those windows. Or rather, over the house that encased them. On a house-hunting trip in June 1998, we looked at fifty or sixty houses. They were all too plain. Or too small. Or too big. One lemon yellow center-hall colonial with black shutters was beautiful in the photo; it turned out to be the lone house sitting in a narrow triangle between a gas station and a highway. Terence returned discouraged to Atlanta to close out our house there; I stayed at work and continued the hunt.

One evening the agent called, excited. Just as twilight began to fall she and I pulled up a nondescript driveway leading up to a garage door and a long cedar walkway. We opened the door and found ourselves suddenly looking out into Oregon itself. Soaring cedar trees framed the view straight down into the Willamette Valley and the river below. Off to the left, flat-topped Mount St. Helens, which had twenty years earlier covered the neighborhood with volcanic ash; off in the distance, the peak of Mount Baker. And there, filling up every window in every room in the house, looking like Mount Fuji, was white-capped Mount Hood. The house was cleverly built into the side of a mountain; the entire front of the house was glass. I called Terence, breathless. "We have to buy this. Now."

The following weekend he flew out to sign the papers. Excited, I walked him through the house. The big bedrooms. The playroom. The cedar decks hanging out into sheer nothingness over the valley. As we stood, the sun went down behind us, turning the mountain in front of us orange, and then pink, and then a misty gray. The lights below us reflected on the river. He was quiet. His body language was noncommittal. He turned away from me. He walked through the rooms, saying almost nothing.

What's wrong?

Nothing.

What's wrong?

Nothing.

He was silent. Not hostile. Just gone.

I was frightened. I didn't understand what was going on. I was racking my brains. What did I do? What did I say?

Have I said something wrong? Talk to me.

Nothing.

He was silent through dinner. Finally the truth dawned on me. He had been in Atlanta alone for a month while I was working here in Oregon. He didn't want to tell me he didn't want to move into this house with me.

"You're having an affair!" I was close to tears.

His mouth opened into a large O.

"It's Alison, isn't it?"

"What are you TALKING about?"

"You won't talk to me. You won't look at me. There's something wrong and you won't tell me. You're having an affair and you don't want to tell me, right?"

"Are you out of your *MIND*? You think I'm having an *AFFAIR*? Are you *CRAZY*?" He spoke in super italics. "It's the *CHRISTMAS TREE*, you dumb broad. The *CHRISTMAS TREE*!"

The Christmas tree?

"There's no front window. This house faces *BACKWARD*. Where am I going to put the Christmas tree? You have to see the Christmas tree from the street. How am I going to live in this house?" His despair was palpable.

The mountain. The eagles. The decks. The sunset. The lights on the river. They all meant nothing. The picture of home in his head was all Jimmy Stewart and *It's a Wonderful Life*. A bay window. A twinkling tree. A fireplace beyond.

"Don't you know anything? The Christmas tree *HAS TO* go in the front window."

Besides, he said, Alison is a dingbat.

Perhaps, I now reason nearly two years later, when he comes home from the hospital we can drive out to the bridge, look across the river and up at our house hanging off the ridge, and see our tree blazing down from a distance. Maybe it will feel like a front window on the world, and Daddy will be cheered.

Together the children and I try to figure out everything we can to make Daddy happy. Terry gets a fuzzy blanket. Georgia finds his slippers. The three of us go to the local animal shelter and pick out the softest, fluffiest, purringest kitten we can find. Terence has wanted a cat for years. Time now for me to give in. On Christmas morning, we put the yowling box under the tree.

Perhaps we are lulled for a time by the gentle terminology the doctors use before they know for sure what they are seeing. When my dad was diagnosed with colon cancer four years earlier, the doctors carefully explained about the "lesion." Although he dutifully went to every appointment and every scan, my mother later reported that it was weeks before my Harvard-educated mathematician father even realized that "lesion" meant cancer, and that he had it.

Terence and I are the same. It is hard for us to get too worked up about a "shadow" or a "cyst" after what we have been through. Everything we have, and our friends and family have, is going toward getting Daddy fixed and getting the children through Christmas. My sister shops for presents and mails them from New York. I buy a sun lamp to make up for the Oregon gloom. Colleagues deliver meals to our door, every day a different dish. Lasagna. Chili. Chicken salad. My mother ships off huge boxes of vitamins. I shower the children with showy and distracting gifts—a Barbie house for Georgia, edgy CDs with previously forbidden lyrics for Terry—and we all shamelessly abuse the terrified cat with affection. On Christmas morning Terence sits immobile in the Daddy wing chair, wrapped in layers of quilts. We bring him Christmas dinner on a tray and, as we do at the end of every day, hold hands and thank God we are together again.

Years later when Terence talks about those weeks, he will barely focus on Christmas, or the cat (who instantly takes a dislike to him) or the dinner, or the view or the tree. What he will remember is the dieffenbachia by his chair.

It is a plant he bought and cared for. In the melee, I have forgotten about it. Terence will recall sitting and watching the plant parch and die, knowing that he needed to get up and water it, or tell someone else to water it, but unable to muster the resources to do so.

If Dr. Turner's office hadn't called on December 26, I am sure we would never have thought about the cancer again.

Three days later, on Friday, December 29, four days after Christmas, two weeks and two days after Terence's colon surgery, we appear in Dr. Craig Turner's office, summoned there by that phone call.

Dr. Turner is young—we guess thirty (he's actually thirty-nine). We later joke about letting children do such important work. Sturdy and handsome, he could be anyone's idea of a TV doctor— a kind of a Dr. Kildare with a surgeon's swagger. It's rather endearing. It's just enough to tell us that this is a man who is confident of his own abilities.

Terence tacitly makes his usual naming bargain: You can be Dr. Turner to me, but I'm MR. FOLEY to you. Even in pain, totally dependent, he doesn't bend his formal, Midwestern 1950s principles. He doesn't have any truck with informality—this whole first-name-on-first-meeting nonsense. MISTER Foley. DOCTOR Turner. The way it is supposed to be.

Yet without any discussion, it is clear that both Terence and I place total trust in this young man. Do we have a choice? What do we know about kidneys or cancer or centimeters or scans or surgery?

He talks about the "cyst," which he tells us the scan has shown to be 7 centimeters in size, about the size of a large garden slug. His notes from the time use the words "very concerning" and "worrisome" and say that he will likely recommend that the kidney be removed.

Another scan on the second day of the new year ("suspicious for carcinoma" reports Anna Gail, M.D., who charges $695 for the scan, and another $100 to read it). A second opinion from a Dr. Kaempf. It is a punishing three weeks for Terence, as debilitated as he is from the removal of his colon.

As for me, those weeks blur into a haze of work, kids, and doctors. My family is nearly three thousand miles away. We have almost no close friends nearby. Sandy, my boss, hovers, motherly. Her husband, Gerard, takes the kids for McDonald's; a colleague's wife picks them up for a movie; a family down the street with four children absorbs Georgia into their midst. I even remember making one desperate phone call. "You and I have never met. Our sons are friends. My husband is ill. Can Terry spend the night?" I am so busy holding things together that I'm barely anxious at all. We have just solved one of Terence's major health problems. Now we are going to solve another.

When I was in high school, a friend was in a severe car crash on the way to a birthday party. As the emergency workers and ambulance techs carried off the injured amid blood and glass and police and noise, she was frantic about the cake. "Don't let the frosting slide off," she kept repeating. January 2001 is a car wreck, and I'm focusing on the cake.

The operation on Thursday, January 18, to remove Terence's kidney is long—more than five hours, according to the bill for the operating room. I have become a connoisseur of waiting rooms. Providence Portland, in downtown Portland, seems older and dingier than its sleek Providence St. Vincent cousin off in the suburbs. I see a woman crying off in one corner. Young adults who appear to be her children huddle around her comforting her. I wonder what news she has just received. The cafeteria is not as plush as the one across town. The coffee doesn't seem as good.

Dr. Turner emerges flushed and triumphant from the operating room, and I am summoned to a tiny consultation cubicle. He is still dressed in scrubs. The operation has been a success, he says. He has removed the diseased kidney, and has done so laparoscopically, through a tiny hole in Terence's abdomen. His recovery will be much faster and much less painful than it might otherwise have been, Dr. Turner says. He has sent the tumor off to the lab—he calls it a tumor this time—for looking at it up close, it appears almost certainly to be cancer. An hour or so later, I am allowed in the recovery room. Terence is lying under the bright lights. "You are going to be fine," I tell him. He is too drugged and groggy to register what I am saying. "Everything is going to be fine."

Dr. Turner is right. The operation is physically less taxing than his earlier one; Terence is released from the hospital just three days later; on January 25, just a week after surgery, Terence is well enough to be brought into the doctor's office. At his visit, Dr. Turner tells us that the cancer is an odd type. "Of unknown origin," he says. He tells us that he'll call just as soon as he knows more.

Still, he is reassuring.

"We got it all," he says.

Terence tears up.

"Thank you for saving my life," he says. They shake hands. Terence never sees him again.

5

My memory is clear on just how much Terence and I had riding on that operation. Until I track Dr. Turner down again, I have no idea what it had meant to him as a young doctor.

Twelve days shy of a decade after the operation and three years after Terence died, I fly out to meet Dr. Turner in Oregon. I have faxed him the pages of his notes and records. When he calls back, he is excited. He remembers Terence. He remembers us both. He remembers Terence's kidney. He's done hundreds of operations since that day, yet he remembers this one very clearly.

What I want to know from Dr. Turner is this: Was Terence's thank-you for saving his life misguided? Was it the romantic and wishful sentiment of a frightened and deluded couple? How badly were we mistaken at the time, in thinking that the operation had "cured" Terence's cancer? Had Dr. Turner been sending out some other, more subtle message that we had—willfully or accidentally—failed to hear?

Not at all, Dr. Turner says. In fact, he is surprised to hear that Terence has died. The literature on kidney cancer is very clear. On average, he reiterates, if a small tumor is removed before the cancer has had a chance to fling its microscopic cells into the bloodstream and implant other places, then surgery can be considered as close to a cure as possible. At 7 centimeters, Terence's tumor was just on the edge.

I also learn from Dr. Turner just what an opportunity Terence presented him at that moment in his surgical career. Terence was very ill. His insides were still roiling from the intestinal surgery just two weeks earlier. Another major surgery would be debilitating. I remember how Dr. Turner explained to us that he would try to remove the kidney through a small hole, to spare Terence the pain and weeks-long recovery of a cut. It was a relatively new technique, he says.

Had I known just how new the surgery was and how new Dr. Turner was to it, my waiting room time would have been completely different. As it is, it isn't until I look over the medical records I have collected that I realize I have no idea how we even got to Dr. Turner in the first place. A polite note in the file from Dr. Turner thanking Dr. David Luallin for the referral is the only clue. Dr. Luallin is the surgeon who removed Terence's colon. But how did we get to Dr. Luallin? I honestly don't know. Perhaps Terence knew. I doubt it. What a level of blind trust we had! We did more research before picking out our real estate agent.

What Terence and I didn't know was that Dr. Turner was new to Oregon. He had just arrived six months earlier, in July. He was also pretty new to surgery, having just finished his residency at University of Chicago. He'd done fewer than twenty such surgeries himself. And he was eager to make his mark. As a resident, he had been working with other doctors on what they called "minimally invasive surgery" back in Chicago, mainly working with living kidney donors. "I drove the camera," he says. But hardly anyone had been doing this kind of surgery for something as big as a kidney here in Oregon at that time. Dr. Turner really wanted to do it. "I wanted to do something cool," he tells me now. "I wanted to be out there pushing the envelope. I wanted to be the guy. That was common for us early surgeons."

I can't say I've ever thought of surgery as "cool," but listening to the excitement in his voice as he recalls operating on my husband almost convinces me. I hear in his voice the same confidence that we saw on his face those many years ago. A kind of professional pride that I can admire. An intellectual curiosity and taste for adventure that I know Terence could have related to—if he could somehow have gotten past the idea that these are HIS guts, and this is HIS life.

Dr. Turner now tells me that Terence's surgery would be by far the most complex he had done. "This was a chance to do something innovative again," Dr. Turner recalls. "It was a great challenge for me to step toward. It was a cool surgery, and the benefit of the extra work was going to be huge." Of course, he adds, in a phrase I am comfortable hearing only at the distance of years, "I was still developing the technique on how I was going to apply it."

I now think Terence would be excited to know how he helped advance the technique. I am glad neither of us knew at the time.

Dr. Turner tells me something else that I am glad Terence and I didn't know back then: He had met many of the people working with him in the operating room that day for the very first time. And that wasn't unusual. As a surgeon, he has his own company. He doesn't work for the hospital. And when he comes to do surgeries he, like other surgeons, doesn't get to pick his own team. The scrub nurses, the attendants, even the anesthesiologists are all assembled anew for each operation.

I know that professionals can come together and work effectively bound by nothing more than their years of common experience. I watch Terence's pickup Dixieland bands perform in just that way. Would I have been happy to know that Terence's complicated surgery was being handled, not by an experienced and well-rehearsed team, but by people who didn't know one another? I think not.

In any case, Dr. Turner says, although tempers can sometimes run high when these professionals' work styles clash, nothing of the sort happened during Terence's surgery. It all went smoothly and well.

The Blue Cross records I've gathered show that the bills for that feat were relatively modest—just over $25,000. Most of that is for the hospital—$1,944 for the room; $124 a day for oxygen; $10,000 for the use of the operating room. Dr. Turner bills $2,590.

As I begin to think about all that we have done and all that we—or someone—has spent to keep Terence alive, a test keeps popping into my head: Would you have paid for this if it had been your own money? That sum—$25,000—is more than half the cost of this year's college tuition for Terry. It's just about what my sister spent to turn her back porch into a comfortable family room. I have a friend who spent twice that for a new kitchen. Would I spend $25,000 for a shot at keeping Terence alive for five years? Damn straight. As it turns out, we paid $209.87. The rest was covered by insurance—in reality by my employer, who footed the bill.

Looking back, I find it astounding how little we knew both about the surgery itself, and about how much it cost.

Instead, our focus was on the bullet we dodged. Terence and I went home to sleep it all off.

6

I return to work at *The Oregonian*. When Dr. Turner calls again, his voice is still upbeat, but his message is not. Terence does not just have an ordinary kidney cancer. He has an extremely rare form of kidney cancer called collecting duct carcinoma. Dr. Turner tells us that he is still optimistic, but we should probably look into this.

In my tiny office at one end of the newsroom, looking out over Southwest Broadway, I tilt my computer screen discreetly away from the door. I am an editor. My fingers can be moving on the keys and I can seem to be working on some story. In reality, I am deep in the Internet.

Kidney cancer is a tiny subset of all cancers. As I click away, I learn from the Kidney Cancer Association website that no one really knows what causes kidney cancer. In terms of who gets it, though, Terence might as well have had a bull's-eye painted on him. Male? Check. One hundred sixty men will get it for every hundred women. Older? Check. He's sixty years old, exactly the average. Overweight? Check to that too, despite both of our best efforts. Smoker? He and I both quit in the mid-1980s, in preparation for Terry's arrival. That is more than fifteen years ago, but it still leaves thirty years of puffing in his past.

In one regard we seem to be lucky. Like many cancers, kidney cancer can just cruise along silently, not causing anyone any trouble, until it suddenly starts causing a lot of trouble, and it's too late. Bleeding. Lumps. Pain. The symptoms that suggest the tumor has broken through its own shell and is invading the body. Terence has

none of that. Like about a third of his fellows, he is fortunate enough
to discover the cancer while we are looking for something else. For
kidney cancer in general, Dr. Turner is right—the signs do seem
encouraging. The cancer hasn't spread. That is the key. I look at one
site and then another. I do the calculations once and then all over
again. It always comes out the same. A sixty-year-old man with a
7-centimeter kidney tumor that hasn't spread anywhere else has
more than a 90 percent chance of making it for five years. Five
years is as far as they are willing to project. That seems like forever.
I'll take it.

But collecting duct cancer? That's a different story. I have to go
deep into the Internet to find anything at all. I scour every site I
can find. I can find only about fifty cases anywhere in the literature. Fifty. That's 0.00000667 percent of all the cancers in the
world. I download research papers. The biggest study I can find is
from Japan, involving only a dozen or so people. Almost all the
other reports are of individual cases, and all come to the same
conclusion: an aggressive tumor with poor prognosis. I search on
the authors' names. I search on the university names. In the lulls
between stories, I call everyone whose name I can find on a paper
or a study. I'm a journalist. I call people. That's what I do.

Most of the people I reach are just pure researchers and, while
they are kindly and sympathetic, they know nothing about the
actual disease or how it could be treated. The oncologists I call
have either never even heard of the cancer or at most have heard
anecdotally of a case or two. The same words keep popping up
over and over in the studies: Rare. Aggressive. Most of the patients in the papers are dead within a few months of diagnosis.

I wander out of my office feeling dazed after hours of research.
My next-door neighbor is another editor, Jack Hart. He's famous
around the country for teaching storytelling techniques to jour-

nalists. He's also a man of precise habits and Teutonic bearing. He has a decidedly unjournalistic discipline. My stories flap loosely and wildly to a deadline crash landing. His stories march tightly to an early finish and are laid out days ahead of time. My team pulls caffeinated all-nighters to finish. His team goes home to dinner. He walks with his shoulders squared. His desk is paper free. Looking at his computer screen once, I thought his email was broken, till I realized I was seeing something I had never seen before: an empty inbox. He deals with his correspondence immediately and then deletes it.

With my head full of the research I have just done, I wander aimlessly into his tidy office intending to ask some trivial question on a story we are both involved in.

"How's it going?" he asks.

I have held it together for my children. I have held it together for Terence. I have held it together for my sister, my parents, the doctors, our friends. Suddenly I am sobbing so hard I can barely stand up. The thought that I have held at bay floods me: What if Terence does not get better? Jack kicks the door shut with his foot and holds me until I cry myself out.

Ten years later, I discover how Dr. Turner arrived at his diagnosis. In the documents I have collected after Terence's death I see the signature of Dr. P. Holbrook Howard on a January 23, 2001, lab report. I have never heard of Dr. Howard. Terence died without ever thinking about him, or knowing the role he played in our lives or Terence's illness. Nor did Dr. Howard know my name, nor did he know how Terence lived or that he died, or that Terry and Georgia are about the same ages as Caitlin, Chelsea, and Madeleine, his three daughters.

Yet in 2001 Dr. Howard peered deeper into Terence's cancer than anyone else and signed off on a terse, three-paragraph message that lay behind Dr. Turner's meeting with us, and that informed, educated, directed, illuminated—and confounded—all of us for the rest of Terence's life.

No one was keeping Dr. Howard a secret back then. It's just that no one thought to mention him. Dr. Howard was the pathologist at Providence Portland who first identified Terence's cancer for what it was. Why would anyone have mentioned him to us? Looking over the records I realize that there are hundreds—maybe even thousands—of similarly anonymous people who touched our lives.

As, a decade later, I examine the notes of our final visit with Dr. Turner, the surgeon, on January 25, 2001, I realize that he was reading from Dr. Howard's pathology report—and that the picture was more complicated than it first appeared. Dr. Howard speaks on the page in a language that to Terence and me might as well have been Greek. After Dr. Turner called with the words "collecting duct," I remember that Terence and I futilely pored over these words for clues:

LEFT KIDNEY: Sections of the kidney show extensive necrosis within which several small foci of viable neoplasm are found. None of these foci impinge on the capsule and no neoplasm is found at the ureteral or vascular margins.

The neoplasm is composed of cells of small to intermediate size with moderately pleomorphic nuclei that vary threefold in size. There is polynucleosis with nuclear grooves and lobulation. Many of the nuclei have small but distinct nucleoli and/or chromocenters. The cells are arranged in a solid pattern with fenestrations.

Immunohistochemical stains show that the neoplastic cells are positive for keratin 7 and vimentin. They are negative for CD10 and CEA.

On January 6, 2011, a decade after those words were written, I decide to go find their author.

I wish Terence were here with me as I head out to Providence Portland hospital to meet Dr. Howard for the first time. I decide to make the trip the way Terence and I would have made it ten years earlier, starting from the driveway of our house.

The towering cedars are still there, now even taller than before. The garage door that Terry and his friend Michael ran into with their skateboards has been repaired. I peer around the corner. Georgia's playhouse is gone. Yet here is the sweeping view I remember, far out to the mountains and the horizon. Terence was right. The house turns its back to the street, and to me. The view is beautiful, but there really is no way to share a Christmas tree with the rest of the world.

I don't know how the drive to these hospitals lived in Terence's memory. I suspect that when he was sick he was focused inward and didn't notice much at all. He entered one hospital in great pain through the emergency room, and the other facing a life-changing operation. I remember these days as sensations, long stretches of super-speed blur abutting moments when time seemed to stand still and I became aware of every fleck of lint on a doctor's coat, and every snag in the fabric of the waiting room sofa. I wonder if, returning, he would have the same reaction I do now. Would it surprise him, as it does me, that the journeys we made then with the sensation of having our fingers in a light socket are in reality so prosaic?

Would he realize that the scary trips are really perfectly ordinary jaunts past a Fuddruckers and a Home Depot and a Bed Bath & Beyond?

Before I go to meet Dr. Howard at Providence Portland, where the cancer was removed, I take a detour over to Providence St. Vincent, on the other side of town, where the cancer was discovered. Would Terence find it amusing that on this return trip I know instinctively—from all the practice a decade earlier—that, as I enter the Providence St. Vincent hospital grounds, I can drive past Mother Joseph Plaza to the *second* parking garage and find a spot in 1-C, next to the bicycles, bypass the elevator, and walk straight through to the West Pavilion?

The hospitals are like small cities, brick and khaki mazes with populations twice the size of Portland when the hospitals were founded. Today at Providence St. Vincent I eat lunch in the cafeteria where the children and I ate dinner every night while Daddy lay upstairs. The ice-cream machine is gone, but the grand piano is still there, pushed back against the wall. Every night when we visited there I remember feeling that ours was the only family in the world, that Terence was the only husband, and mine the only story. Today I see an orderly in blue scrubs and running shoes help himself to barbecue pork and coleslaw and, with a casual boredom, pick a bag of chips from a wire rack. Watching him, I realize once again that my unique story is his workday. All day long people with stories like ours are coming and going through these workers' lives. These are, after all, just hospitals. Ordinary hospitals.

Despite their sprawling size, neither hospital is huge, as hospitals go. Yet together they provide the livelihood for 7,648 people like that orderly, people who come to work here every day, park in the lots, eat lunch in the cafeterias, exchange small gifts at holiday sing-alongs. Each of the patients who sleeps here each night after gallbladders are removed, lumps excised, broken bones set, and new children ushered into the world helps 7.6 other people raise their families, pay their mortgages, and visit Disney World. And they're just a microcosm of the millions of people around the country doing pretty much the same thing day in and day out. Checking blood pressure. Looking into eyes and ears. Taking blood.

I head back across the city to Providence Portland, where Dr. Howard badges me past the door that says "Authorized Personnel Only." Hundreds of patients enter the hospital every day, thousands every year, brushing past Dr. Howard's world but not realizing he's there, discovering the truths that will influence the lives of patients and their families.

The lab is relatively quiet. In the evening, after samples collected around the state begin arriving by FedEx truck, the lab warren becomes an assembly-line factory, as technicians settle in for the night to shave micron-thin slices of tissue, fix them on slides, and apply reagents and antibodies to fluids. The machines and people work all night. Trained eyes peer through microscopes. Assistants prepare reports, bringing good news, or bad, to anxious patients.

It is here, into this tangle of microscopes and slides, technicians and trays of tubes capped in purple, gold, magenta, and red, that a sliver of Terence's tumor made its way.

Dr. Howard runs the whole lab today; back then he was in charge of only a section of it. Today, I can tell that he and Terence would have enjoyed talking to each other. Dr. Howard was a biophysics and history major at Amherst with a Sunday night campus radio show—he still has a tape of an interview he did with Henry Steele Commager. He looks like a geek, yet his office is a jumble of kites and bobbing-duck barometers, and topographical maps; on the door is a photo of him on a motorcycle. When he was a kid he wanted to be a geologist. Or an astronomer. He settled on pathology because he wanted a place "at the cutting edge" of science.

Sitting on his desk today are the nineteen slides, arranged neatly in a cardboard tray, all labeled: Terence Foley/Case #P01-922. We take those slides and walk down the hall to a double-headed microscope where we can look at them together. For all the space-age, stainless-steel, digital-flashing aura of the lab, the basic technology of pathology hasn't changed in over a century, and the basic tool is still the eyeball.

I learn that on one level, a pathologist's work is very exacting. A chunk of the tumor is fixed in formaldehyde to keep the cells from disintegrating and then locked into a block of paraffin to preserve it. For each set of tests, a thin slice is shaved off and stained. Without the stain, Dr. Howard says, the cells appear like ghosts on the slides. The nucleus is stained a dark blue, almost purple.

Eosin, a fluorescent dye, then stains the membrane and the thick liquid of the cytoplasm. Then with the contrasting stains, you can clearly see the cells and their nuclei and their shapes.

As he would have back then, Dr. Howard today first trains the microscope on a slide from a normal spot on Terence's kidney. He lets me look at these cells. They are a placid pink, flat with gently undulating edges. The tiny flecks of eosin-stained blue that are the cells' nuclei are widely spaced and regularly placed. The whole impression is of calm and order.

Then Dr. Howard switches slides. This slide has a piece cut from the middle of the tumor. I focus the eyepiece. My vision fills with tiny blue dots—hundreds of cells' nuclei—randomly and angrily jostling against one another.

"Ants!" I say, surprised.

"Ants," he agrees. "It's how I would describe it to a class of residents: chaos in the anthill."

Even I can see that something is wrong with these cells. There are too many nuclei, too many cells. They are pushing and shoving against one another. They have broken ranks. They are disorderly.

Dr. Howard moves the slide slightly and I can see a single cell frozen in time, stopped in the process of dividing. Surrounding this chaos—just alongside the anthills—are cheerless blank pools of calm, not the calm of the normal cells, but an eerie pale nothingness. This is the necrosis—the cell death—that he mentioned in the report to Dr. Turner. That morning in 2001 when Dr. Turner removed the tumor during the surgery, the cells were growing so fast that they were outstripping their own food supply and dying almost as fast as they were being born.

I'm not sure what I am supposed to feel now. Am I supposed to be horrified? Disgusted? Sad? In reality, I am fascinated. I think Terence would have been fascinated too, yet caught between two emotions. He hated anything abnormal or strange or gross. He banned all medical talk at dinner. So perhaps these views of his own malady would have frightened or revolted him. On the other hand, he loved knowledge. Any kind of knowledge. I can picture him with his ever-present stack of index cards taking detailed notes, imperiously slowing down the conversation until he got the spelling right. And me? The thought that pops into my head is uncouth: "So you are the little bastards who killed my husband!"

The cancer part is clear. That's not hard. Even my civilian eyes can see that Terence had cancer. But collecting duct cancer? What is that?

Together Dr. Howard and I peel back the layers of the story of what happened next.

As Dr. Howard takes me behind the scenes to discussions that took place unbeknownst to Terence and me, a weird contrast emerges. From back in the past I remember the adamantine certainty Terence and I both wanted from the lab report. What did he have? What would it do to him? What should *we* do? Even the words "lab report" promise an objective reality.

Yet today as he talks to me, Dr. Howard is very clear himself that while the science is precise, the conclusions are not. "It's a standing source of amusement—or bemusement—among pathologists that if you take a team of ten world experts and give them each ten slides from a breast cancer and see how often they agree, it's disappointingly low. In borderline calls, they are all over the place," he explains. "It shows that we're always looking for black and white, but things are often shades of gray."

I learn that one way of distinguishing cancers is simply by looking at the shapes and characteristics of the cells. Another way is by seeing how they react when different antibodies are applied.

Dr. Howard does both.

The most orderly, sensible method is through a kind of flow chart that plots an orderly course of action—an algorithm, he calls it. Do the cells react to this? If so, then do this. If not, do that, and so on in a predictable pathway until a picture emerges and he gets an answer—or runs out of options and must make a call without knowing for certain.

If he's in a hurry, he can do a lot of tests at once, but that's more expensive. Each of the antibodies costs from fifty to one hundred dollars; the more targeted the approach, the fewer the tests he must do, and the cheaper it will be. "The sisters"—the nuns who manage the hospitals—"run a tight ship," he says. He applies one antibody. In the presence of this antibody, a "garden variety" kidney cancer will turn brown. Terence's cells did not.

Dr. Howard shows me the ghostly pale slide from Terence's stained tumor side by side with the much darker one from a known ordinary kidney cancer. All that proves is that Terence's cancer cells weren't of the common variety—and that's the source of Dr. Turner's statement to us in the first meeting that the cancer was "of unknown origin."

That's as far as Dr. Howard could take the analysis back then. Even his lab—a big lab, inside a big hospital that does tests for other hospitals all over the state—can't afford to keep rare antibodies around that will be used only once or twice a year. So he didn't have access to the more specialized substances that would be needed to test the tumor further.

As for the economics of testing, Dr. Howard knows only the cells and the science. He doesn't know which patients pay and which don't, or whether the people whose cells he is testing have insurance or not, or what kind. He didn't know—nor did Terence and I know at the time—what the hospital billed for the tests or what the insurance companies paid, or how anyone arrived at any of these numbers. His job was to figure out the ailment in the most efficient way possible, not to figure out how to pay for it.

Dr. Howard's tests back then were inconclusive. He wanted to know more, so he turned to a more specialized lab. On January 25, 2001—the day Dr. Turner talked to Terence and me—Dr. Howard sent the slides to Dr. Allen Gown, at PhenoPath Labs in Seattle, where some of the hardest cases in the country make their way.

So now I drive up I-5 to Seattle, a three-hour drive from Dr. Howard's Portland office.

PhenoPath Labs is right where you would expect a start-up to be, in the Fremont section of Seattle, a funky gentrified Haight-Ashbury kind of neighborhood. Adobe, the software company, is nearby. So is Google. Wooden-front stores with handwritten menus sell cappuccino, cinnamon lattes, organic food, and running gear. A pathway looks out over Lake Union, and also over the canal that runs from the lake to the sea, passing the blue industrial-looking building where PhenoPath's sixty-five employees work. Dr. Allen Gown rides his bike to work along that path; his helmet hangs from a rack in his office.

Dr. Gown founded the company in 1997, just four years before Terence's cells entered his life. He was a professor at the University of Washington when he chafed at his department's management and decided to strike out on his own—becoming another start-up in the $55 billion testing industry. Just outside his office, a quiet, library-like room is filled with about a half-dozen seven-headed microscopes, so that as many pathologists as possible can look at difficult slides at once. Off to the side, in a darkened, curtained alcove, a doctor is doing a FISH test, a fluorescent test looking for a mutated gene. With this test, pathologists can look deeper into the DNA of cells than was ever possible a decade ago.

In the back room a half-dozen identical white machines turn out to be computers programmed to add dyes and reagents and antibodies to slides. The technicians have named these machines and taught them to make odd sounds when they have finished their tasks. While we are talking, a machine named Isabelle moos. Klarabelle calls out, "You've got troubles!"

"That's so we can tell which machine needs attention," Dr. Gown explains—when they have finished their work, for example. We walk past a white, coffin-shaped contraption. The device sends one cell at a time shooting through a tunnel, so that each individual cell can be examined. "That baby cost twice what my first house in Seattle did," says a technician sitting nearby. I look the machine up online. It's called a flow cytometer. Such machines can cost $75,000, $100,000—even $200,000.

A second technician sits at the computer screen that goes with it, grappling with analyzing the cells from a blood cancer.

The lab at PhenoPath gets the complicated cases. The difficult cases. The ones that other doctors can't figure out, or that they disagree on.

But even Dr. Gown has seen only a few collecting duct cases in his lifetime.

When Dr. Howard sent Terence's cells here, all he knew was what they did *not* react to. That's why he sent them to Dr. Gown: Back in 2001, Dr. Gown had access to more antibodies and more tests. To Terence's cells, he applied an antibody—$34\beta E_{12}$—and the cells turned an angry, positive color. Today he taps a few keys on his computer and the picture of Terence's cells from back

then—a deeply hued abstract of brown, purple, and black—
appears on the screen.

"I developed that antibody when I was a professor at the University of Washington," he says casually. It is now used by pathologists all over the world. "The university makes millions of dollars every year from it," he says. Then he holds up his thumb and forefinger an inch apart: "Full disclosure—I make this much."

Dr. Gown did four tests on Terence's cells, using the antibody he developed, as well as three others. Two tests were positive, two negative, a pattern that led him to conclude that the tumor was indeed of the collecting duct variety. On January 29, 2001, he sent that report back to Dr. Howard, and that is when Dr. Turner called us with the news.

I remember clearly how anxiously Terence and I awaited the report, and how we pored over it for clues. Yet now, in retrospect, I wonder why we bothered. In fact, I wonder why we spent so much time and money—not to mention the brainpower of two such extraordinary men—on plumbing the internal workings of the cell. The tests showed us all what the disease might be. Not what we should do about it.

Back then, very little besides surgery was available to treat kidney cancer. What there was didn't seem to be particularly effective. Chemotherapy didn't work at all. For Dr. Howard, that is one of the frustrations of the job—and was even more so then.

"A lot of what we do is gilding the lily," he says. "It's interesting and very academic, but it's not like I learn something that says I'll reach for this drug or that drug and this will make the difference."

Now I ask Dr. Gown the same question. His answer is similarly cheerfully direct, as I know Terence's would have been if he had been the doctor: We do it for the knowledge. "This may not be important *now*," he says. But it may be important in a year. "There's always the possibility of things happening down the pike. There's always a hope that we'll find a therapy."

· · ·

It's that hope that kept me obsessively prowling the Internet a decade before my conversations with Drs. Gown and Howard. There were tantalizing signs that something was changing in cancer treatment. It was just hard for me to figure out how and where and how it applied to us. Right in our own back yard, Brian Druker, an oncologist up the hill at Oregon Health and Science University, had found a new way of attacking cancers. His discovery—that by blocking certain enzymes you can keep the cancer from dividing—changed everything, but only for a tiny number of people with very specific cancers. His drug—which would be named Gleevec—was still several months from Food and Drug Administration approval. But the Internet back then was already alive with stories of patients whose chronic myeloid leukemia was halted in its tracks by the drug. Dr. Druker's face appeared on the cover of *Time* magazine for turning what was once a death sentence into a chronic illness. Surely there must be something like that on the horizon for kidney cancer.

That was what I was looking for.

"Something is happening out there," I tell Terence at the time. "They are discovering new things all the time." I don't know what that something is, but I believe we will find it. "We will just have to keep you alive until they discover the cure for this. All we need is a few years."

I am blindly optimistic.

I even believe myself.

Just after the operation, Terence and I consider a few extreme possibilities. One article mentions interesting work by a doctor in Paris. We're not even quite sure what he's doing, but we consider— for an instant—relocating. I prowl the biggest cancer centers— MD Anderson in Texas, Sloan-Kettering in New York, Fred

Hutchinson in Seattle. No one seems to know much more than I do about collecting duct cancer.

On February 9, 2001, Dr. Turner takes Terence's file before the tumor board at Providence Portland, where all the hospital's specialists review cases. Because there is no sign of metastases—the spread of the cancer from the kidney to other organs—Dr. Turner's recommendation to the board, and to us, is that we do a chest X-ray to make sure his lungs are clear and then follow up with scans every six months.

Watchful waiting, it's called.

Waiting for him to die is what we feared.

Yet he doesn't die.

He gets better.

We don't know why. We try not to think about it.

It's like the pictures I remember from 1975, the year I graduated from college and the year that the war in Lebanon tore that country apart. I remember photos of women, baskets over their arms, stepping gingerly over the rubble during a lull in the fighting, heading for market.

I think: How much people want life to return to normal!

On February 15, 2001, Terence's chest X-ray comes back clear. He begins to feel better. We gradually put the trauma out of our minds and our routines start to take over once again. Jazz band for Terry. Ice skating for Georgia. Mornings at Starbucks with coffee for me and Terence, hot chocolate and lemon pound cake for the kids. Terence goes back to cooking chili and lasagna, and we resume going to church at the cathedral downtown.

On April Fools' Day, the children and I pull off one of our best pranks ever. Even at his healthiest, Daddy is never at his best in the morning. So we carefully plan to tease him about that fact. After Terence goes to bed, Terry and Georgia and I get up and race around the house, moving all the clocks forward one hour. We change the kitchen clock. We change the alarm clock. We change the clocks on the microwave and the stove. I sneak in and get his watch and move the hands forward. Terry even remembers to go out to the car and change the clock on the dash. The next morning, I shake Terence awake.

"We've overslept!"

He has a meeting to see a man about a trumpet at nine o'clock in Oregon City, across the bridge.

"It's already eight thirty!" I cry, and the kids play along, pretending to be upset about being late for school. Terence throws on his clothes and stumbles out the door.

Several hours later, I get a call at work.

"Very funny."

It takes him a full hour of waiting outside a locked store to realize he's been had. The kids are delighted.

While Terence is sick and recovering, I am coddling, conciliatory. I tiptoe around his moods and try to arrange things the way he likes. As he recovers, the old ways reemerge.

I leave on a trip for several days. His friend Patrick comes to stay. When I return on a Saturday morning, I can hardly push the back door open against all the recycling piled up in the laundry room. Cheerios boxes. Paper towel rolls. Empty cans of tomato paste and red beans. Empty two-liter bottles of Diet Coke. I walk through the kitchen, where dishes—cooking and eating—are piled on the countertops. On the table. In the sink. I spot evidence of spaghetti. Several empty pizza boxes. The garbage cans are overflowing. They clearly haven't been emptied in days. On past into the living room, where unsorted, unfolded laundry covers every surface. Evidently some clothes had not completely dried, because underwear, socks, pajamas, and jeans are draped over the backs of chairs and the sofa and even over the tops of lampshades. As I walk down the stairs to the family room below, I smell the untouched cat litter box.

I find Georgia and Terry in pajamas and Patrick and Terence in their underwear in front of the television set. More dishes and food, bowls and glasses. Several days' worth of newspapers are layered on the carpet. All four of them have colds. There are boxes of Kleenex everywhere, and the floor is covered with crumpled, used tissues, tossed every which way.

I am screaming before I make it halfway across the room.

"You are pigs! Pigs! All of you! You too, Patrick."

They all freeze in place.

"How can you even think of sitting here like this? This is disgusting!"

No one moves.

"Get up. Now. All of you. Get this mess cleaned up. You too, Patrick."

I'm raging.

"Terence, how could you? How could you let them? How can you even sit here in this pigpen?"

Finally Terence reacts.

He becomes furious.

With me.

His face reddens. He outshouts me. The old Terence is back.

"You told me you were coming home Saturday *night*!"

7

In the last week of May 2001, Terence, at age sixty-one, finally gets his Ph.D., completing the degree he began in 1957.

I see in the history of that degree a zigzag, ebullient path of almost dizzying choices. Books. Music. Friends. Adventure. Mystery. Travel. Language. Study. I peer back with amazement into the kaleidoscope that was his life before me.

He spent only one semester in college when he was seventeen, a tuba player in the famous Ohio State University marching band. Even today mail from TBDBITL—The Best Damn Band in the Land—comes to the house addressed to him. It has followed him for fifty years, past his death, through at least twenty-three address changes in three countries and nine states that I can count.

After that came the navy, and his stint in the Philippines translating Chinese radio transmissions of ship movements. He mystified his friends with hints of all the things his security clearance prevented him from saying. When he left the navy, he reinvented himself again—this time as a radio announcer in Xenia, Ohio.

Sometime in 1966 something pulled him west, and soon the cable car conductors and brakemen of the San Francisco Municipal Railway Company began to hear rumors of the new guy working the cars who spoke Chinese better than the Chinese.

Today as I stare at the picture of him grinning out the back window of cable car number 509 in his conductor's uniform, I think I know what drew him there. In the photo, the car is suspended at a gravity-defying angle. Over Terence's shoulder Hyde

Street drops down to the San Francisco Bay. The view from the Powell-Hyde line stretches out across the bay. Alcatraz is below. Off in the distance, Angel Island.

Even now I can see him clearly as he was back then, twenty-six years old, in the uniform vest, jacket, and tie, a six-slot steel change belt strapped to his waist, flirting with the young women on their way to work as they jump onto the wooden steps. In my imagination, I can see him leaning into the wind and reciting Tu Fu's eighth-century laments of loneliness that I know he has already come to love.

> *Red clouds tower in the west*
> *The sun is sinking on the plain*
> *A sparrow chirps on the wicker gate*
> *I return from a thousand li away.*

I can see him, lurking unseen one afternoon behind a Chinese family frantically arguing over the itinerary.

"Xiage zhan, zai xia che," I can hear him say, as if it is the most natural thing in the world: Wait till the next stop, then get off, he is telling them. I can see his glee as the Chinese family starts as if a dog has spoken.

Even back then Terence was already painting fanciful pictures of his dark past, hinting at secrets he could tell if he chose, wives and children left behind and mysterious trips to places no one else had visited. His friend Dick Epstein, himself a brilliant odd-ball wanderer, worked as a gripman on the same cable cars. He remembers even then the whispers that Foley was a spy.

Dick and Terence shouted and argued about the things young people shouted and argued about in the 1960s. The war. The economy. Marxism. Communism. Capitalism. The military-industrial complex.

On and on they argued until one day they stuffed their savings into their pockets, jumped off the cable cars, and headed to Europe, and then on to crisscrossing the Soviet Union. Moscow. Novgorod. St. Petersburg. Vyborg.

It wasn't until after that trip that Terence in 1969—by then twenty-nine years old and married—developed a hunger for school again. He threw himself into his studies as if some vacuum at his core needed to be filled up with all the learning in the world. Years later, boxes in our basement were filled with all his college notes in his round, easily legible handwriting, clipped in old-fashioned red, buff, green, and blue cardboard binder covers.

Modern Korean history. Japanese philosophy. Chinese politics. Modern Japanese literature. Medieval Chinese history. Japanese foreign policy. Even after nearly forty years his notes would remain clear and coherent. They include details about the third-century scholars who formed literary clubs—the most famous of whom were named "The Seven Sages of the Bamboo Grove." They drank and discussed metaphysical problems long into the night.

No wonder the China we both knew disappointed him so!

His notes reveal the world he built for himself from his studies, a world as romantic and crazy and eccentric as he, a world that he could live in happily.

Still, he was restless. Partway through his master's degree, he threw it over and moved to Vermont. For a time, he and his wife lived in a converted Vermont schoolhouse with the anthropologist Margaret Mead, whom he befriended at Columbia. He worked in a prison. He got a job with state government promoting Vermont agricultural products around the world. He moved to Missouri. He learned soybeans. He traveled to China and met me.

Twenty years later, impatient and brisk, I badger him into diving back into his studies to finish his Ph.D. We are living in New York again, just blocks from Columbia. I am working and writing books. He wants to go to law school. He wants to start an import-export company. He wants to write a novel. He wants to go to medical school.

"Why don't you finish your Ph.D. first?" I ask, part supportively, part as a challenge, part irritated at his mercurial mind.

And so he does.

His studies go with us wherever we go. They follow us as we push the stroller down to the dinosaur playground in Riverside Park; as we move to Atlanta and throw the kids and the dog into our pool; when we move to Oregon and pitch our tent on the rainy and foggy side of Mount Rainier and build fires from damp wood. All the while he is chipping away at his degree.

Little by little the thesis takes shape, and as it does, he weaves his own years in China into a case study about the cultural barriers to foreign cooperation.

Finally, at the end of May 2001, it is finished. We are living in Portland, but Terence and I and the children fly to New York for the ceremony. We stay in the Plaza Hotel. We walk through Central Park up to Columbia University on the far Upper West Side. At noon at Columbia University he will defend his thesis and have his Ph.D. at last. At noon on the same day, about three blocks away, I am also at Columbia University, with my newsroom team as we receive a Pulitzer Prize for the work we did on the Immigration and Naturalization Service in those hectic final months of 2000. I am sitting at the table amid a happy group of journalists as Terence walks in.

I jump up.

"Meet Dr. Foley!" I cry out to the assembled group.

He pulls at the hem of his suit jacket, and curtsies.

We have lived three years in Oregon. On Sunday afternoons once a month we drive up to the Milwaukee Elks Lodge, nestled between City Auto Wholesale and a shop advertising windshields for 50 percent off. Nothing much appears to have changed at the club since it first opened in 1956.

Terence plays here once a month with the Portland Dixieland Jazz Society. "Muskrat Rag." "After You've Gone." "Canal Street Blues." His tuba holds down the bass line. Sometimes he sits in on string bass. Georgia and Terry eat hamburgers and chicken fingers and fries in the room with the upholstered white bar and the brown Naugahyde stools.

We hope that the bad times have passed.

Our time here is drawing to a close. Soon the whole family will be packing up and leaving again. I have been offered my own small newspaper in Lexington, Kentucky. As the Oregon summer gets older we drive out near the base of Mount Hood for the last time, to pick blueberries and raspberries and marionberries. In the car on the way home, Mount Hood looming off to our right, the four of us sing silly rounds, ending up with "Sloop John B," weaving in and out of the melody and backup, laughing with pure pleasure when we nail the last chords.

Early in September 2001, we again prepare to move. Terence leaps at the adventure. This time it is he who will go first. He will leave two days early and get the children into school, I will stay behind to finish up my work and close up the house. He's still not strong enough after two operations for a long walk with bags, so we arrange a wheelchair for the long trek between terminals in St. Louis. Otherwise, he is fine. He calls me, pleased, from our new home. He and the children spend the day filling the house with food. Everything is ready and they will be so glad to see me.

In the middle of the night I take a dark peek into the world that Terence must have been living in. By myself in the silent house in

Oregon, my family 2,400 miles away, no one nearby to realize I am alone, I awaken feeling as if an elephant is sitting on my chest. My arms and legs are leaden. There is a band around my heart pulling tighter and tighter. I cannot catch my breath. I call an ambulance.

A few days later, everyone will conclude that the chest pains are simply the stress of the past six months finally coming to rest in me. But thus it is that on September 11, 2001, at 9:03 a.m. EST—6:03 a.m. in Portland—Terence is in the principal's office in Lexington, Kentucky, registering our children for school and I am lying on an emergency room gurney in the hospital where I spent so many days with Terence, as we each look up at a TV screen to see the second plane crash into the World Trade Center.

8

If Terence's vision of a proper 1950s family life has a stage set, it is here in Lexington. Modest brick houses line the streets, and proper steps lead to proper front doors. The front windows look out over sidewalks and neatly trimmed shrubs and lawns. A young girl clutching a violin case passes our house every morning on her way to school. We hear children laughing over our back fence. The roots of tall oak trees push up ridges in the walks, the kind we both remember catching our roller skates on.

The house we rent until our own is ready reminds us both of the places we grew up. The kitchen has yellow appliances and a beige linoleum floor. In the living room, bookshelves flank a white-painted brick fireplace. Our bedrooms are tiny, clustered around a small center landing and a single bathroom with porcelain fixtures and white tiles. We can all hear one another breathe in the night. We play Monopoly and Life on the dining room table.

I settle in to the world of news in Kentucky. I learn about horse breeding and become obsessed with the mystery disease that makes mares miscarry and just-born foals die. Abuse of the powerful pain-killer OxyContin continues its fatal sweep of eastern Kentucky. Lovely old racetracks agitate to add slot machines to compete with casinos. I try to understand the manic grip that Tubby Smith's sixth-ranked college basketball team has on the region. There is a vague, uneasy sense of war off in the distance, heading toward us.

Lexington is only ninety miles from Cincinnati, the town of Terence's childhood. We drive up and look at the old neighborhoods, once genteel, then rough, now bohemian, where Kentucky and Ohio come together at the Ohio River. Terence tells the children stories of his life as a musician in the bars here. Terry is turning into a musician himself. We reluctantly let him crowd-surf his first rock concert. Georgia is becoming a rider. Every Saturday Georgia and I drive out Old Richmond Road to Champagne Run, where she coaxes forty-year-old Dan over foot-high jumps.

Terence becomes director of a new Asia Center at the University of Kentucky. His shirt pockets bulge with index cards covered with thoughts—musings on cars, politics, history; vocabulary words in Spanish, Russian, Chinese, Japanese, German, French; funny things the children have said; recipes for chili and lasagna. Nearly three years after his death I will be moving something and see an index card covered in his handwriting drop to the ground. The card is covered with ideas for the new center.

Life is good.

On Monday, May 6, 2002, I am at my desk at the *Herald-Leader* preparing for the news meeting to lay out the front page of the next day's paper. It is a slow day. Fans are camping out waiting for *Star Wars II: Attack of the Clones.* Storms are rolling in. The phone rings. It is Terry, with panic in his voice.

"Mom, come home. Dad is sick."

I find Terence in bed, his face flaming with fever, shaking with chills under a pile of blankets. He can barely speak.

"Terence—what's wrong?" I'm frightened.

He looks away. "It's a reaction to some medicine."

"Medicine? What medicine?"

He won't meet my eyes. "I wasn't feeling well so I got some medicine . . ." He is shaking some more.

My voice rises a notch. "What's going on? TELL me! You have to tell me."

His teeth chatter. His face is red. Sweat is pouring off him, yet he is shaking as if it is winter. He tries one more time. "I had a cold…so I…"

Now I panic. "Terence, this is bullshit. Tell me. NOW."

He gives in.

"The cancer is in my lungs. I have six to nine months left."

His lungs!

What?

My fingers and toes leap with electricity, the electricity of fear.

I have felt a shock like this only once before in my life, at nineteen years old when I rode my motorbike around a blind curve straight into an oncoming car. The car hit me, the motorbike fell under the wheels, I rolled over the hood and my shock said the same thing then as it is saying now: This cannot be happening. On that winding road in France thirty years earlier, however, the shock instantly resolved into bemused acceptance: "Oh, shit. I'm going to die. What a pain."

This time, lying on the bed beside my shaking husband, the shock does not resolve. I have been holding the fear at bay for more than a year now. With this one instant, it explodes inside me and I can barely breathe or think.

Over the next hour he pants in bed beside me. Sweat soaks the bedclothes. Little by little the story comes out.

Dr. Turner had advised scans every six months, to monitor any possible spread. I remember the first one, the previous April, and our relief when it came back clean. Without telling me, Terence had the second one here in Lexington. Alone in a radiologist's office at St. Joseph Hospital on February 12, 2002, Terence saw the faint dusting of flecks in his lungs. Two weeks later, again alone, he had a second scan. The records from this visit call them "nodules, highly suspicious for metastasis."

More than two months went by as he kept his secret. He went to work. He came home. We read, played games with the kids, drank wine, had dinner with friends. He found an oncologist, met with him, planned a course of action. He said nothing to me. I suspected nothing.

Yet, with this revelation, some odd behavior becomes clear. He has been packing up things and sending them off to friends. Cameras. Books. Paintings.

"I have too much stuff," he told me. In retrospect, the sentiment is so bizarrely improbable I wonder how it escaped me. What betrays his secret is not the illness, however. It is the medicine.

Without telling anyone, the oncologist and he together decided on a treatment. The side effects of the injection that Terence took in the morning are already kicking in.

What was he thinking?

He wanted to spare us, he explains. If the treatment succeeds, and he is cured, then we never have to know how close he has come. If—as he expects—the treatment fails, he will at least have spared us months of anguish. He even has been plotting to prepare us for the inevitable. He planned to stay at work a little later every night—without mentioning anything to us, of course—so that we would gradually get used to life going on without him.

What was he thinking?

I am exasperated, shocked, annoyed, horrified, amused, pained, incredulous.

And very, very, very touched.

Even in this, he is acting so much like himself. How could he carry this burden alone for so long?

"Did you think I would just not notice if you didn't come home one day?" I ask him. I lie with him until, exhausted, he finally falls asleep.

In the bedroom next door, Terry is sitting quietly. Now he calls me. In an older-than-thirteen voice he asks me, "Mom, is there something you should tell me?" I make a quick assessment. He needs to know what I know. He doesn't deserve to hear what I fear.

"Dad's cancer has come back. He's got a good doctor, and we are going to do everything we can to keep him well," I say. He is troubled but asks no more questions.

9

Throughout that night, I sit alone in our dark living room.

Everything has depended on Dr. Turner's "we got it all." I also remember him saying that if we made it a year past the surgery, chances were good we would be home free. We made it through sixteen months. Bad as the cancer is, rare and unknown as it is, everyone seemed to agree that if it was cleanly excised, we would be safe. If some particles escaped, no matter how tiny, we would be doomed.

They have escaped.

Everything is different now.

Just as in an old movie, the lightning bolt of that recognition lights up the landscape of my life. Sitting alone that night, I suddenly see everything as a negative of itself, the reverse image of the way it appeared before.

In my mind, we had tamed this cancer into an annoyance. All at once I see it for what it is—a killer. After the shock of Terence's surgery, the future again seemed endless and any reckoning far away. Even with the cancer in our past, when I thought about our days ahead, if I thought of them at all, they still seemed like tissues, popping up to use as I pleased and discard at will. The lightning bolt reminds me of what we know but have ignored till now, that these days have a number. Now, I suddenly realize, tomorrow may be today.

Fear freezes me. For with this reverse-image picture comes a stabbing sense of anticipated loss.

In the nearly nineteen years since we collided in China, we have settled into a feisty but loving accommodation. Our fights have ends now, and our disagreements resolve. We find more to like than dislike in each other. Still, in the press of ordinary days, we spend much of the time grappling with the things that annoy, things that need fixing, things that trouble or disturb. Why can't you pick that up? Why did you say that? Can't you stop doing that? It is no longer the angry and aggressive battering of two strong-willed people. It is instead the mindless daily scrabbling of two harried parents.

Yet in one second, that lightning bolt shows me the things I have ignored.

It shows me what I will lose if I lose him.

All through that dark Kentucky night, as Terence lies upstairs asleep, I am awake downstairs. The future grows foggy with my fear, the past reshapes itself. As I reprise memories, I see things I have forgotten, or have never seen before.

In the middle of my memories of conflict and strife in China, I suddenly discover the memory of another dark night, when, almost paralyzed with anxiety over some recrimination from my harsh boss, I am similarly unable to sleep. Terence rises from our warm bed and, bundled in a People's Liberation Army greatcoat, walks me around and around nearby Ritan Park until dawn when I can finally collapse, exhausted.

I remember him screaming at his boss; I had forgotten his invective at mine. "She can't talk to you like that!" he rages. "You're twice as smart as she is!" His anger makes me believe, for a moment, in my own strength.

I remember days in New York when, indignant at his strong views and his refusal to yield, I slam doors. Yet tonight my memory retrieves a different, long-buried moment: It is afternoon in

the city and we are walking down Broadway when, without warning, he hip-checks me into an open doorway and I fall. I look up
in fury just in time to see three figures, guns drawn, charge past.
Terence is standing between me and them. He is bossy. He is
pushy. Without a second thought, he puts himself between me
and danger.

As night turns to morning, I realize more clearly than ever before how much over the years I have come to see myself through
his eyes. The moves I would not have made. The chances I would
not have taken. I leave a job that has been my home since college.
I pack up our house not once but three times. Sometimes he infu-
riates me with his insistence that I can do the things I fear doing.
He never backs down.

Tonight as he lies upstairs, the memory of our early trip to
Florida resurfaces. Only this time, in the light of the electric
shock of my fear, I see something I have long forgotten about the
alarming, crazed would-be helicopter pilot I married. My memory refocuses, this time not on him but on me.

There I am. I am sitting in the open door of a Cessna. I am
wearing a yellow helmet and red sweatshirt. A smile freezes on
my face. Behind the smile is pure terror. While Terence is pursuing his quixotic quest to get a pilot's license in four days, I head
off for my own adventure.

As soon as I sign up at a nearby skydiving school, I regret my
impulsive choice. I am afraid of flying, so the whole endeavor is
weirdly masochistic. I want to quit but I am too proud to back
down. After a half day of training, the instructor straps me into
the chute. I am almost sick with fear. We prepare to taxi. I think I
may faint.

As I look out the door of the plane, suddenly he is there. I don't
know when he arrived, or how he has found me, but there he is, in
his burgundy windbreaker and newsboy cap. He looks at me in a
way that I have never seen before, from anyone. I see pride. Deep,

unadulterated, unabashed pride. He knows I am terrified. He knows I am going to go through with it anyway. And he is proud of me. He snaps a photo. He waves.

As we climb over the same blue and green landscape he navigated the day before, I think: I am doing something new. Something brave. Something fun.

I am flying.

I step out the door of the plane into the wind. I hold on to the wing above my head and brace my feet on a tiny ledge. I throw myself backward into the air. Suddenly, everything is still and quiet, and I am hanging from the sky. He is there when I land.

Alone in the dark sixteen years later, I realize for the first time that this crazy man doesn't just believe he can fly.

He believes that I can too.

I resolve two things that night.

The first is that I will never let another day go by without telling him how much I love him, and how much he means to me and the children.

The second is that I cannot let this happen.

I cannot just let him die.

10

Two days later, on May 8, 2002, I accompany Terence to his next visit with Dr. Scott Pierce, the oncologist who has been secretly treating him.

Dr. Pierce is a general oncologist, the kind you find all over the country on the front line of everyone's everyday cancers. He sees breast cancer and colon cancer and skin cancer and leukemia. He administers chemotherapy and radiation and advice and comfort. I flinch at the sight of the sick people in the waiting room, the turbaned women and men with canes and walkers.

A nurse calls us to an examining room. After a few minutes, Dr. Pierce opens the door. He spots us both sitting there.

He raises his eyebrows. "So you told her?"

Terence nods.

I have a fistful of printouts. Names of doctors. Names of hospitals. Names of drugs and descriptions of clinical trials. I thrust them at Dr. Pierce.

He looks over at Terence.

"This is who you were protecting?" he asks.

Terence looks sheepish. He shrugs.

"Guy's a head case," I say.

Dr. Pierce looks at Terence again.

Terence shrugs again.

"She may save your life," Dr. Pierce says.

. . .

For the next six weeks, Terence continues his treatments. As he and Dr. Pierce have agreed, he gets daily injections of interleukin-2, a type of hormone that stimulates the body's immune response to fight off invaders like cancer. For reasons no one seems to understand, the chemotherapy used to blast many other kinds of cancers has little effect on kidney cancer. Interleukin is naturally found in the body and helps fight infections; sometimes it even has to be suppressed—for example, when a patient is undergoing a transplant. About a decade before Terence met Dr. Pierce, the FDA approved the synthetic form of IL-2 to treat kidney cancer and melanoma. In some cases, for reasons no one completely understands, the injections can cause the body to rise up and beat back the tumors.

There are two ways to administer IL-2. Patients choosing the high-dose method are confined to intensive care wards and given intravenous drips every eight hours. This method has some real promise: In one study, 7 percent of those undergoing this treatment had their cancer disappear, at least for a while. I read further, though, and realize that this is a game of Russian roulette. Four percent of the patients in the same study died from the side effects of the treatment. One hundred chambers in the gun. In seven chambers, something resembling a cure. In four, live ammo. No one knows who will get which. Point the gun at your temple, and fire.

The low-dose version—the kind Terence is doing—involves a shot every day. Same drug, lower intensity. The side effects, although less dangerous, are the same. Fever. Chills. Shaking. Diarrhea. Nausea. Vomiting. It's like suffering a violent flu and malaria at the same time. But even low-dose IL-2 apparently offers some promise: 15 percent of those taking it will respond, the brochure says.

Terence begins going to the office at Bob-O-Link Drive first thing in the morning, to get the shot over with before he goes to work. But we quickly realize that the terrible symptoms begin about six hours after the injection. If he gets the shot at 9:00 a.m., then by midafternoon he needs to be helped home from the office. We switch the appointment from first thing in the morning to last thing in the afternoon. If he gets the shot at 3:00 p.m., he can make it through dinner before the shaking begins.

It is not enough. The Asia Center is in frenetic start-up mode. Terence struggles to get himself to work as often as he can. But on some days at 3:00 p.m., he is felled by the shaking. On other days, he must leave the office early for the shots. On many days, even the best days, he falls asleep sitting up, the victim of sleep lost to chills, fever, and vomiting. Reluctantly, he resigns. His job at the Asia Center thus becomes the first casualty of his illness, and of our quest for a cure. He never works full time again. He is sixty-one years old.

Later that week, I visit a therapist.

"I can't survive without him," I say.

"What does he say when you feel this way?" she asks.

"He says I can handle anything."

"You'll need to say that to yourself from now on."

Alone with Dr. Pierce, Terence had just learned he was going to die. Perhaps soon.

What was that moment like?

Seven and a half years after he and Terence met I fly back to Lexington to visit Dr. Pierce. He has moved from his office on Bob-O-Link and now has a much smaller practice, his office looking out over a parking lot. He sees me in his office after 6:00 p.m., when all his patients have left. He still has a couple of hours of dictation left to go. He will return to his wife and children after eight, as he does on most days.

Dr. Pierce remembers Terence well.

"I can still see him," he says. He wore a trench coat. He wore a fedora. "He was a very interesting man."

During the clandestine meetings back then, before Terence let me in on the secret, they discussed Terence's options. Dr. Pierce explained the odds—that the average length of survival after a kidney cancer metastasis is six to nine months. Terence's reaction surprised him.

"The first thing he said was: 'Doc, do you have any female patients who have recently died? I need to find a widower so my wife can meet her next husband,'" Dr. Pierce recalls. "I've never had anybody say anything like that before."

It doesn't surprise me that Dr. Pierce has never before had a patient ask a question like that. Nor does it surprise me now that Terence asked it. Having looked after him for all those years, I now know for certain why the first thing he would think about would be to look after me.

11

Throughout the summer of 2002, after Terence and I leave Dr. Pierce's office, I research interleukin-2 as thoroughly as I know how. I discover the Cytokine Research Group. I look up papers in obscure journals. Scientific papers compare high-dose interleukin to low-dose. They compare interleukin to interferon, a similar protein. They compare interleukin to nothing. They are nerdy publications—important to the progress of science, I am sure, but maddeningly useless to me. They compare drug pathways, molecular structures. There are papers that I think of as the "Lourdes reports" that describe unexplained cases of spontaneous remission following some unlikely treatment.

There are papers whose titles I can't even fathom, like one from the *International Journal of Clinical Oncology*, published five years before Terence's diagnosis:

Clinical efficacy of adoptive immunotherapy by IL-4 activated tumor-infiltrating lymphocytes in patients with advanced cancer

Or one from the *Annals of Surgical Oncology* in 1994:

Induction of lymphokine-activated killing with reduced secretion of interleukin-1β, tumor necrosis factor-α, and interferon-γ by interleukin-2 analogs

What do these mean? What can I learn from them? My head spins. Making it even more confusing, almost all the papers have studied the most common version of kidney cancer—clear cell cancer. There are almost no references anywhere to the rare and mysterious collecting duct cancer, so we really have no reason to know one way or another if anything will work on Terence.

Still, some of the papers I download seem encouraging. They talk about "response rates" and they seem to be saying the same thing that Dr. Pierce and the drug's maker are saying. Some studies say the "response rate" for IL-2 in kidney cancer is 8 percent. Some say 15 percent. Some go as high as 23 percent. There are weird abbreviations. CR. OR. PR. DR.

After a bit I tease out the code: Complete response. Objective response. Partial response. Durable response. All good. These various categories are measuring whether the tumor reacts to the therapy. Does the tumor shrink? Vanish? If so, for how long?

The more I read, though, the more puzzled I become. I understand that having the tumor shrink is a good thing. Perhaps a very good thing. But what I care about is not Terence's tumor. It is Terence. I want to know if anything is going to make him live longer.

And so I scour the papers one more time for answers to the question I have most on my mind: So how long do these people live? If they take the IL-2 and the tumor shrinks, do they live longer? If so, how much longer?

The papers are mysteriously vague.

I find one paper from 1993 that suggests evidence, but not proof, of longer survival. ("How long? *HOW LONG?*" Frustrated, I begin shouting at the papers themselves.) I am not a skilled scientific researcher. The terms confuse me.

Instinctively, I understand that it is easier and faster to measure the way the tumor responds—a scan every three months can provide a comparison, while survival is so much more complicated to figure out. Yet I am sure I must be missing something. Isn't survival the point? Why will none of these papers tell me how much longer this treatment will make my husband live?

It isn't until I go looking again nine years after our meeting in Dr. Pierce's office that I find references to studies sharing my frustration. I find a Canadian group that tabulates fifty-three studies totaling 6,114 patients and concludes that tumor response doesn't correlate very well with survival at all in kidney cancer patients. Did we suspect that even back then? I have no idea.

Now, in the fall of 2009, I sit across the desk from Dr. Pierce. I want to know: Why IL-2? Why did you and Terence make the choices you did?

Dr. Pierce's simple answer: That's all we had.

There are two kinds of patients who come to him, he explains. One kind wants to be left alone, to know as little as possible, to be confronted by as little as possible, to do as little as possible. This might be someone who is old, who is already at the end of a long life. Someone fearful. Or, very likely, someone in tremendous pain from an advanced case.

Terence is none of these people. He is only three-quarters through the life he expected. He is still relatively healthy other-wise. He is not in pain. He has a young family. He wants Dr. Pierce to fix him. In this, Dr. Pierce says, he is like most people.

"I know that he wanted to get better. Who wouldn't?" Dr. Pierce says. "He would have been willing to do anything. I think most of us would be that way. He may have been a unique human, but he shared the emotions of most. It's strange the hell people will go through to keep living," he says. If not for themselves, they "maybe live for their wife, or children or grandchildren."

Before interleukin-2 was approved in 1992 to treat kidney can-cer, Dr. Pierce had nothing to offer. With interleukin there was at least a chance. Dr. Pierce, and Terence, both know it was a slim chance. It was a chance nonetheless.

In fact, for Dr. Pierce, the pain of the job comes from just how empty his hands often are.

People like Terence—and me—"want you to come up with anything possible. I will run out of ideas and they'll still be standing there looking at me, saying, 'What can you do for me?'"

As for money, Dr. Pierce is more aware than most of the strange conflicts that insurance and Medicare impose on doctors like him. The reason he is in a smaller office now is because of a 2005 change in the way Medicare reimburses doctors for chemotherapy drugs. Oncologists make much of their income essentially "selling" chemotherapy drugs to patients, with Medicare paying the doctors higher prices than what it costs the doctors to buy the drugs they are administering. Back in 2005, Medicare cut the amount it reimbursed. Many doctors switched to prescribing drugs that would earn them more money.

Did that affect the drugs he prescribed?

"The physician's cash cow is chemotherapy," he says. "You really have to be ethical." It cut into his income and he downsized his office.

Dr. Pierce is also more aware than most of what insurance coverage—or the lack of it—means to patients.

His practice is in the relatively well-off university town of Lexington. Yet like all doctors and hospitals in Lexington and Louisville, his office is a magnet for patients from all over the region, including the desperately poor Appalachian eastern part of the state. He muses about a recent patient, a woman recovering from breast cancer surgery. There are two drugs she can take to reduce the risk of her cancer returning. One is an aromatase inhibitor, a relatively new kind of enzyme blocker that will cost three hundred dollars a month. The other is tamoxifen, an older drug that Dr. Pierce says she can get at Wal-Mart for three dollars. The more expensive drug is, in Dr. Pierce's estimation, about 20 percent more effective. Four thousand dollars a year. Twenty percent greater chance of keeping a cancer at bay. She doesn't—can't?—do it.

12

What makes me think curing Terence's cancer is my responsibility?

What makes me think I can find things the doctors can't? It's not just hubris, I tell myself. I'm not completely crazy. I have seen other people—one a dear friend, the other a longtime colleague—both thread the needle of despair and almost certain death and emerge on the other side with a cure. My friend was snatched from dying of AIDS by a chance introduction to a doctor who prescribed an experimental antiviral cocktail. The colleague beat leukemia with a cutting-edge bone marrow transplant. Both were told they were at the end of their lives. Both arrived at their cures only through mighty research, bravery, and luck.

I'm smart, I'm strong, I'm brave, I tell myself. If I try hard enough, I can save Terence too.

But how?

In search of the answer, I become part of a cancer community.

Terence always maintained that Americans are joiners. For every imaginable human activity—and for some that defy imagination, he said—you will find a group with a president and a board of directors. They will have meetings and newsletters and agendas and jealousies and a certain amount of huffing that not all members are equally pulling their weight. Whatever these organizations are, they will have T-shirts that say "WHATEVER—and proud of it!" And bumper stickers that say "I ♥ WHATEVER."

One day in New York Terence set out to prove his theory. During the early 1990s, when Terry was a baby, and before Georgia entered our lives, we planned surprise excursions for each other—a day at a sculpture garden, a nighttime picnic at the Cloisters, chocolates and a bottle of champagne on the ice at Rockefeller Center.

"Dress up!" Terence commanded one Saturday morning. "Terry too." He was already in a nice business suit. We were heading for the day's surprise.

I put on a dress. Stockings. Heels. Even a little makeup. I shoehorned three-year-old Terry into a nice polo shirt and slacks. We piled into the car. We headed east across Manhattan, over the Triborough Bridge, past LaGuardia Airport and off into Long Island. We drove for a long time. We can't be heading for a theater, I thought. We wouldn't be taking Terry to a theater. It must be some wonderful new restaurant Terence has discovered. Something ethnic. In a quaint neighborhood. We both like that. We exited the Long Island Expressway and began twisting through environs that had seen better days. We pulled into a parking lot behind a dingy VFW hall. Terence headed to a desk just inside the door and bought three ten-dollar tickets.

Inside the hall was a massive, three-state show of canaries.

Birds.

The hall was filled with rows of caged canaries. Bright yellow domestics. Fluffy white ones. Birds with amazing pointed crowns of feathers. Canaries that sat silent in their cages and ones that sang out across the room. There were Lancashires, Yorkshires, Spanish Timbrados. There were birds in onyx and brown, Venezuelan Black-Hooded Red Siskins, German Rollers, Persian Singers, Russian Singers. We roamed the hall, amazed at the variety.

Terence was smug. There, on the table just outside the main hall, was living proof of his theory: T-shirts. A newsletter. Bumper stickers. Canary Breeders Make Better Lovers.

Canary breeders. Kidney cancer. For everything there is a community. And, by the time Terence is diagnosed, there are not only bumper stickers and T-shirts. I find on my computer that there are listservs.

Kidney-Onc, the online gathering place for all things kidney cancer, was a pretty dreary place when I first briefly peeked into it back in Oregon in January 2001. Like all such forums, it is a kind of online conversation among dozens, sometimes hundreds, sometimes thousands of people. Yet even though people have been regularly gathering here to chat for nearly five years, few seem to have any more ideas, or options, than I do.

As I look back over the postings from the first two months of 2001, I see people asking questions about a German vaccine, about antiretroviral treatment, Shaklee vitamins, stem cell transplants, antioxidants, mushroom compounds, a tantalizing reference to "anti-VEGF" compounds, a man whose wife is about to be treated using the anti-AIDS drugs Viramune and Epivir, and one query about the acne drug Accutane as a possible cause of, or cure for, kidney cancer.

Fourteen months later, just after the dark lonely night when I pondered the cancer's return, I am searching for what to do now. I log back into the community and find that something is different.

The group is still behaving as Terence said that any group will: There are leaders—RobinJoker, a knowledgeable and opinionated contributor, has posted information on the site 1,700 times since Terence's operation. There are followers—"I'm new here" reads a common subject line. There is a group language: "Uncle

NED!" reads one post, which turns out to be excitement that the last scan has found "No Evidence of Disease." There are hurt feelings. "Take me off this List NOW!" commands one person, upset that someone in the group has questioned her choice of treatment. There are even the T-shirts Terence predicts. They read "SCAN THIS" and are offered by one of the group's members.

What is different about the Internet group in May 2002, from January 2001, is the range of treatments people are discussing— and subjecting themselves to. There are still lots of references to things that—even to my hopeful eyes—seem improbable. A post on the usefulness of cruciferous vegetables and a vegan diet. One on vitamin B_{12}. The report from someone whose disease has stabilized after a laetrile treatment at a clinic in Mexico.

Now, however, there is also chatter about clinical trials of a whole variety of oddly named compounds.

Some of these trials must have been going on all along. Suddenly the conversation is getting louder.

With the benefit of hindsight, it is easy to pick out the proper pathway from the clutter. Several patients talk about a trial of CCI-779 that they are beginning; that drug later will become Pfizer's Torisel, used against difficult kidney cancers that respond to nothing else. There is chatter about bevacizumab, which will become Genentech's Avastin, which Terence will eventually use on trial.

Yet in 2002 they are just part of the stew. They don't stand out. Avastin bumps up against cryoablation—freezing the kidney cancer in place using radiation. Torisel is discussed right next to stem cell transplants. Patients on the listserv are being treated with radiation. Thalidomide. Interferon. Alone. In combination. In high doses, in low doses. In trials. In offices. In hospitals. People are taking drugs that work against one cancer—Iressa, Tarceva— and trying it against kidney cancer too. Patients swap doctors' names like trading cards. We compare hospitals. Where should we go? Whom can we trust? We all pore over the list. Is this doctor for me? Does this drug show promise? Should I try it? Should I switch what I am doing? Can I thread the needle? Can I push the bell curve?

How much money are people spending on this chase? It's hard to tell, although the topic is never far from people's minds. There are endless online discussions of insurance coverage and Medicare rules. One man asks the group for help: Should he spend $350,000 to enroll his sister in a trial of stem cell transplants in Seattle? One talks about trying to talk his insurance company into covering $2,500 a week for the same kind of IL-2 treatments Terence is getting. One asks the list for help figuring out how to import Anzemet that his aunt is taking for nausea now that her insurance company has stopped covering the hundred-dollar-per-tablet cost.

A man in Pakistan reports on his dad's treatment using a Texas doctor's protocol: "If this may be of any interest to you guys I just wanted to report and 'accurately' that the four drug combination cost of interferon, thalidomide, capecitabine and Coumadin is coming to Rupees 73000 total per month ie in Dollars 1200. And this is the total cost." He goes on. "These meds are all being imported to Pakistan and it is very interesting to note that obviously these meds are not as expensive to manufacture as they are being sold in the United States." He asks: "I wonder what's the profit margin???"

The group on the Internet is in general very friendly. I email one man and he writes back immediately with detailed information. I ask a couple about a program in Texas. They respond offering me their guest room. Amid all the noise, though, one name stands out for me, because the woman who calls herself lmodrngrrl—who turns out to be a modern furniture dealer named Laura Lear—is writing about her boyfriend, who has collecting duct cancer! What's more, as I scroll through the history of her postings I discover that they have settled on Gleevec as a treatment for him—the very Gleevec that I had been looking at back in Oregon. And it seems to be working! I find a message she posted in February 2002, after Robert had begun taking the drug:

The last week has been each day better than the one before. He has regained his appetite, is doing more each day, is less and less tired, looks better than he has looked in a year, and today I just couldn't believe how "normal" he was at work. This is very unusual for us as Robert has been very sick.

Excited, I contact her, and on May 12, 2002, I post a message myself for the group.

Hello—

I've just finished cruising several years' worth of archives, and notice that there are several of you who are diagnosed with collecting duct carcinoma. My husband had a radical nephrectomy in January, 2001, and the diagnosis was collecting duct. His first scan in August, 2001, was clear. His second scan, in February, 2002, showed numerous small nodules on his lungs. He's now being treated with IL-2, low dose. We were given the standard "13-month mean survival time" speech, and that there isn't much more than IL-2 that can be done. But after cruising the Web for two days, I'm up for trying a lot more than that. We've registered at MD Anderson, where I see there is an open RCC clinical trial of some antiangiogenesis agents. Also, based on Laura's experience with Bob, I am requesting that his slides be retested. Also on the advice of Laura, I'm looking into Gleevec. I would like to be in touch with anyone else who is dealing with collecting duct cancer, as I can see that there is very little firm knowledge about it. I'd like to learn from

your experience, and also share my own, as I am prepared to go into
full research mode. Laura—I sent you a private email, but if you see
this first, I'd love to be in touch.
   Thank you!
   Amanda Bennett ·
   wife of Terence Foley
   diagnosed 12/00
   radical neph 1/01
   mets to lung 2/02
   currently on IL-2

Looking back at that post today, I am struck by two things. One
is how quickly I adopt the coloration of the group, with the little
abbreviation-studded biographical tag at the end. The second is
how startling the date is in retrospect. The date of the posting—
May 12, 2002—is only six days after our son's frightened phone
call to me. I've gone into hyperdrive.

Seven years later when I pore over Dr. Pierce's medical records
from those days, I can re-create my own frenetic path:

May 22—foley returns accompanied by wife. She has found about
six different protocols. One involves c-kit, others chemo. One
considers use of iressa and another with vascular growth factor
inhibitor.

Over the next five months of notes, there are references to a
request to look into angiogenesis inhibitors. Another request for
a "battery of tests" at a specialized lab in Illinois, and then later
the results of those tests. The tests show that Terence's tumor is
positive for the protein HER2/neu, which makes breast cancers
more aggressive. That makes him a candidate for the breast cancer drug Herceptin. I seek, and get, approval from the insurance
company to try that drug too.

. . .

Behind the scenes something is happening that I—and perhaps most of the people in the Internet group and even their doctors—won't fully understand for years to come.

For decades all cancer was treated pretty much the same way: Cut it out. Bombard it with chemicals—chemotherapy—or try to burn it with radiation.

For kidney cancer, IL-2 was a new pathway, working off the idea that the body's immune system could be harnessed to help fight the cancer. Now something new is happening, as a twenty-year-old concept begins to be tested in earnest. Tumors depend on angiogenesis, the process by which they build blood vessels to feed themselves and grow. Cut off their blood supply and the tumors will shrink and die.

Or so the theory goes.

Without really understanding why, I sign Terence up for a trial of an antiangiogenesis agent, the idea being to stop the flow of blood to the cancer.

Deep, deep behind the scenes something else is happening that I won't know about for another decade: A powerful antiangiogenesis agent called SU11248 (so named because it is the 11,248th compound tested) has been sent around the world. A doctor in France, throwing the same kind of hopeful spaghetti against the wall that I observed happening to my friends on the listserv, gives it to some kidney cancer patients, whose tumors begin shrinking. Somewhere, somehow out there people are pushing the bell curve.

The dean of the Internet discussion group, and the chief bell-curve pusher, a man named Steve Dunn, exhorts everyone to push the boundaries. Do not be afraid of the bell curve, he says. Do not be afraid of the median. He himself found his kidney cancer at the age of thirty-two, in 1989. He is still alive in 2003, four-teen years later.

On his personal website, he posts an article by Stephen Jay Gould, a Harvard biologist who was diagnosed with abdominal mesothelioma in 1982 and was told he had a median survival chance of eight months. He thinks: The median means half will die before eight months and half will die after. But HOW LONG AFTER? Nothing about that eight-month median says whether that "after" will be eight months and one day or eight months and thirty years. The small tail of the bell curve stretches out into the unknown future.

This is the part of Gould's article that stuck me: "I saw no reason why I shouldn't be in that small tail." I see no reason why Terence shouldn't be there, too.

As it turns out, Terence himself makes all my research irrelevant—for the moment at least.

He continues the interleukin-2 injections for seven weeks, bearing up under increasing fatigue, nausea, and fevers. Finally, he cannot stand it anymore. On June 26, 2002, he takes his last dose and quits.

I don't blame him a bit. The side effects have been awful. What's even more awful: The drug has had no effect whatsoever. The cancer is still growing.

Later, after his death, I will review the insurance records showing that each time he was treated with IL-2 from May 6, 2001, to June 14, 2001, it was billed at $735 a dose. Twenty-four shots, $735 a dose. $17,640.

No effect.

For the rest of the spring and summer of 2002, eight-year-old Georgia rides her bicycle up and down the shaded sidewalks of South Ashland Avenue. Terence returns, not quite to normal, but close. He begins to teach Chinese history at a nearby community college. He is exuberant about the music clanging up from the back stairs. Thirteen-year-old Terry and his friends Shannon, Hughes, and Tanner form a band, Point Taken. Our basement becomes their headquarters. They practice with a fierce discipline and enter a battle of the bands. They come in last. They are nonetheless excited. They have competed against *high school* students!

"It's my dream," Terence says over and over again. "Someday we're going to gig together."

The truth is, we are both still shaken at Dr. Pierce's news and the failure of the interleukin-2.

"What would you regret dying without having seen?" I ask Terence one evening. His mind must have been turning in the same direction as mine. He answers without hesitation.

"Pompeii."

By October, the kids are well into the school year. Yet without a second thought we pull Terry from his eighth-grade class, Georgia out of third, and fly off to Italy to see the excavated remains of the city once buried under volcanic ash. We stay in a whitewashed bungalow, perched high up on a cliff on the Amalfi Coast. Terence and I drink espresso and look down over the cobalt sea to Capri. The tourists are gone. The farmers spread out white cloths and harvest their olives. We drive up the black-lipped cone of Vesuvius that blanketed the coastal city with lava and ash forty-six years after the death of Christ. We walk the stony streets. We poke into frescoed houses, taverns, and baths. We look at shops where busy people on their way home from work two millennia ago grabbed a meal. We sit for a while on the steps of the coliseum where humans pitted humans against other humans. The children giggle at the lewd drawings scratched into the walls and the statues seeming to struggle under the weight of oversized phalluses. Terence maps out every step. I pause near the Temple of Jupiter, taking an eerie comfort from the nearly two-thousand-year-old ash-preserved shapes of families huddled together, trying to ward off disaster.

13

Something terrible is about to happen, *and there is nothing you can do about it.*

Try to conjure that feeling.

An out-of-control truck speeds toward a child. A bridge jumper throws one leg over the rail. A train hurtles at 150 miles an hour toward a school bus stalled on the track. *And there is nothing you can do about it.*

The feeling comes to me in dreams. My babies are in the front seat of our careening car. I am in the back. *And I can't get to the steering wheel or brakes.* Recently I had such a dream: Something terrible is happening to Georgia. I don't know what it is. It is something awful. But I can't move a limb to reach her, or even open my eyes to see her. *There's nothing I can do.* My sister, who is a scientist, says it's only an illusion, caused by waking up in the wrong order, while some of the brain is still locked in REM sleep.

It doesn't change the feeling.

It's how I feel for the next three and a half years. From August 2002 to December 2005, Terence and I do nothing—nothing—to treat his cancer.

Nothing.

We do nothing because a new doctor we have found—a kidney cancer expert at Cleveland Clinic—has told us to do nothing. We have sought out and chosen Dr. Ronald Bukowski ourselves. We trust Dr. Bukowski. We think his advice is right. Even today I think his advice was mostly right.

· · ·

We met with Dr. Bukowski in August, before planning our trip to Italy. On Saturday, August 17, 2002, we packed up the Volvo wagon and drove from Lexington to the Cleveland Clinic where Dr. Bukowski, one of the world's experts on kidney cancer, would tell us what to do next.

Both of us had grown to worship the Beatles, and we visited the Rock and Roll Hall of Fame in Cleveland, marveling at the display of John Lennon's guitars and handwritten manuscripts. We made this a family trip, but really we were in Cleveland to see Dr. Bukowski. I was drawn to one exhibit in the museum—a passage by Yoko Ono describing a bicycle ride she and John and their son Sean take—and I thought: How ordinary their life together seems. In the middle of the room there was something else: Yoko had loaned to the exhibit the glasses John was wearing on the day he was shot. A matter-of-fact line from the exhibit caught me in the gut: After he died at St. Luke's–Roosevelt in New York, they gave her his belongings in a *paper bag*. I think: *A PAPER BAG!*

We haven't abandoned Dr. Pierce in Lexington. The records I collect show that we will have several more appointments with him. Still, like most other family oncologists, Dr. Pierce doesn't see very many kidney cancer patients a year and has never seen collecting duct before. Even Dr. Pierce agrees that Terence's odd disease needs some expert attention.

As I search out the alternatives I am drawn to the famous cancer centers, but few seem to have any special interest in or experience with kidney cancer. Face down in the Internet, I begin scanning scientific papers for names. A few begin appearing over and over again. Dr. Ronald Bukowski is a professor of medicine, medical adviser to the kidney cancer association. He writes papers educating other doctors on kidney cancer. I see his name on studies going back to the 1980s. Clearly he is one of the world's experts on kidney cancer. When we visit him, we realize he is one of the experts on collecting duct as well: He sees six or seven cases a year, almost a flood! Now Terence is one of them.

The Cleveland Clinic waiting room is tan and calm and quiet. Within five minutes of checking in, Terence is called to the back, weighed, measured, and escorted to an examining room. At precisely our appointment time, Dr. Ronald Bukowski swings open the door. He is a stoutly compact man about Terence's age. In another century, his build and full gray mustache might have evoked a prosperous merchant—a butcher, perhaps. In this role, as doctor, what we see in him is confidence. Even before he speaks, we can feel that he carries a certainty in his own judgment. Terence begins to explain that he has come here because he suffers from the rare collecting duct cancer.

"No you don't," Dr. Bukowski says.

We have been in his office for less than five minutes. The doctor's matter-of-fact assurance startles us. We are confused.

What?

How does he know?

"You're sitting here," Dr. Bukowski says. "If you had collecting duct, you would be dead."

Then he reminds us of what should have been obvious: Collecting duct is a very aggressive cancer. I was not wrong more than a year ago when I noticed that everyone in the studies I found died quickly. I figured Terence was lucky. Dr. Bukowski figures he doesn't have what we thought.

Terence and I register the surprise in each other's faces.

Can this be?

Dr. Bukowski sends us off with a list of instructions. More scans. A lung biopsy. More reviews of the pathology. We return to

Dr. Pierce with the news. His notes from that visit say that we are all going to "kind of start from scratch."

By November 13, 2002, we have gathered all the "from scratch" information Dr. Bukowski requested. Terence and I return to his office in Cleveland. The clinic is the same cool, calm beige. Once again, we are called within minutes of our appointment. Once again, at exactly the prescribed time, Dr. Bukowski walks in. We have done the lung scan. The head scan. The needle biopsy of the tiny lung spots, which required an overnight hospital stay in Lexington. We sent Dr. Bukowski the nineteen slides that Dr. Howard prepared two years earlier at Providence Portland hospital in Oregon. I also, as usual, have my personal stash of research to thrust at him.

He wants none of it. He cuts right to the point. As he suspected, he says, Terence does not have collecting duct cancer. Instead, says Dr. Bukowski, he has another almost equally rare variant called papillary cancer. Collecting duct cancer is the most aggressive of kidney cancers. Papillary is the most "indolent," he says— the slowest growing, the opposite of aggressive.

"I recommend you do nothing," he says.

Both Terence and I begin to sputter. I begin to natter about the printouts I have in my bag. The experimental treatments, the clinical trials, the—

"I recommend you do nothing," he repeats. There is that same certainty in his voice. With his words, the fast-growing cancer we fear is replaced by a tamer, slower-growing version of itself. We haven't beaten the bell curve. We have switched places on it.

"I recommend you do nothing."

And so that's just what we do.

Yet doing nothing is not something I do well. As we were growing up, my sister called me "the ant"—able to carry fifty times my body weight without complaint. Terence calls me "the Energizer bunny" and annoys me by following me around the house clapping imaginary cymbals as I hurl orders and lists and tasks. I do four things at once. Terence is constantly rebuking me for paying bills while I am watching movies or for loading the dishwasher when he is trying to talk. For years I have made Terry and Georgia crazy on Saturdays with my ideas and plans and excursions, until I finally realize that I am the only one in the family who sees these vast empty weekend hours as opportunities for accomplishment and self-improvement.

In the biblical story of Mary and Martha, it is Martha I identify with. Martha, who runs around setting the table, putting out the olives, making sure the dishes are clean and the wine and water jugs are filled and there is enough bread for everyone—while everyone else including her sister Mary just lolls around listening to Jesus. I know. I know. Jesus chastises her for bustling and praises Mary's attention. But what does Jesus know? If Martha doesn't do that stuff, then who will? Will he?

It has been only six months since I vowed to do everything I could to keep Terence alive. Now Dr. Bukowski is telling me that the best I can do is nothing.

In retrospect, perhaps we should not have been so surprised by Dr. Bukowski's conclusion about Terence's cancer.

Seven years after that visit, as I dive into the medical records, I find something that I don't remember—if in fact I ever knew it in the first place.

In Terence's medical files I find a letter dated April 9, 2001—more than a year and a half before the visit when Dr. Bukowski told us to "do nothing." The letter is from a Dr. Patricia Troncoso, a pathologist at MD Anderson in Houston, to Dr. Turner, the surgeon in Oregon who removed Terence's kidney. The letter is terse. Only three short paragraphs long:

> *Enclosed please find a copy of our pathology report on the above captioned patient.*
>
> *I have reviewed this case with Doctors Alberto Ayala and Pheroze Tamboli. In our opinion the tumor represents a papillary renal cell carcinoma which is predominantly solid. In some sections focal areas with a more typical papillary architecture with foamy histiocytes are present.*
>
> *Thank you very much for allowing us to review this case.*

Papillary? It's the same word Dr. Bukowski would use a year and a half later after all our "from scratch" testing. I don't understand now how she came to the conclusion she did—I don't even understand some of the words—but I do understand the implication: Behind the scenes, experts were arguing about just how fast Terence was going to die.

When I prowl through the files, I realize that back then even Dr. Turner was startled. In Terence's medical files, Dr. Turner, the surgeon, expresses his surprise at the different diagnosis in a handwritten note addressed to Dr. Brook Howard, the pathologist at Providence Portland who first diagnosed the cancer as collecting duct. The note read: "Dr. Howard: Wow! What do you think? Craig Turner."

So how do we get from "Wow" in 2001 to Dr. Bukowski's different diagnosis, and to our surprise in 2002 when Dr. Bukowski says pretty much the same thing the letter says?

So how did this Dr. Troncoso—a name I don't recognize—get involved in the first place? Even though I don't recognize her name I do remember clearly that her involvement is my doing. Right after Dr. Turner removed Terence's kidney, I couldn't quite believe the conclusion that Terence had such a rare disease. I asked for one more review. I even remember writing the $250 check, and I remember my own suggestion that the slides be sent to MD Anderson. But after that, my memory goes dark.

And so, apparently, does everyone else's. I ask everyone involved and find that what happened next is pretty much lost to time. Perhaps someone called and read us the letter and we forgot? Perhaps someone simply forgot to tell us? More likely, judging from my recent conversations with Dr. Turner the surgeon, Dr. Howard the pathologist, and Dr. Gown, the superpathologist with the mooing machines, this is sort of what happened: At Providence Portland, the pathologist Dr. Howard reviewed the opinion from Dr. Troncoso that I had solicited from MD Anderson. Then, as he did at the very outset of Terence's illness, Dr. Howard consulted the expert Dr. Gown in his Seattle lab. Dr. Gown looked at the MD Anderson methodology, which involved looking at the shape of the cells. Dr. Gown considered his own methodology, which involved checking chemical reactions to certain proteins. He called in another colleague to consult. Together, they all concluded that they were right and Dr. Troncoso was wrong and told Dr. Turner so. Then, I surmise, Dr. Turner called and told us something like this: "There is some controversy about the exact kind of cancer it is, but our best guess is still collecting duct."

Which, of course, was absolutely true.

Best guess.

When I return to Cleveland in 2009 to see Dr. Bukowski again, he has retired. We meet in a small office in a row outside the check-in hall where Terence and I used to await our appointments. Dr. Bukowski has shaved off his mustache and now looks less like a butcher than like the round-faced little boy he must once have been. He has a consulting business. He sits on the boards of some medical technology companies.

I ask him about Terence.

"I remember him vividly," says Dr. Bukowski.

Dr. Bukowski sits behind the desk to answer my questions, still the doctor despite the sport shirt and more relaxed demeanor. As we review the decisions we made together in 2002, I am struck by one thing: Here is one of the world's leading experts on kidney cancer, at one of the world's foremost medical centers. Here is a man who knows all the world's most cutting-edge research, who attends conferences with the world's best scientists. This is a man who looks at my husband and speaks in a clear voice with an un-ambiguous message. Yet the more we talk about what he—and we—did and didn't know in 2002, the more it becomes clear to me that in many ways this disease is every bit as confounding for the other doctors, and for him, as it was for us.

Up until 1995, Dr. Bukowski says—just seven years before Terence and I met him—"we thought that all cases of kidney cancer were alike. They were all treated the same." Dr. Bukowski and I talk now in 2009 about how kidney cancer was treated back then—with interferon and the same interleukin-2 that Terence first secretly tried. Again, I am struck by how closely even Dr. Bukowski's expert experience mirrors our own: If things felt murky and unclear and confusing to us, then that's because they were.

And still, to a great extent, are.

Interleukin-2—IL-2—was first used in the early 1980s. "It's been twenty-five years," he says, "and we still don't know how it works."

What they were just beginning to understand when Terence and I first came to see him, Dr. Bukowski now says, was that the conventional treatment didn't work very well—if at all—on the rare versions of kidney cancer like collecting duct or papillary. Dr. Bukowski doesn't fault Dr. Pierce and Terence for turning to IL-2 in Lexington. After all, it had been the standard of care since it was approved by the FDA in 1992.

By the time Terence was diagnosed in 2001, Dr. Bukowski now says, the information was just beginning to filter out revealing that with Terence's odd cancer—whether papillary or collecting duct—there most likely was zero chance that the painful and awful experience of taking IL-2 would have done him any good at all.

So what about our decision to do nothing, I ask now. Do you still think that was a good choice?

Yes, says Dr. Bukowski. I hear in his voice the same clarity Terence and I together heard back then. And yet as he reviews the confusing state of knowledge back in late 2002 I can see some of the ambivalence that must lie behind the adamantine certainty.

Collecting duct cancer is so different that some doctors even believe it isn't kidney cancer at all—even though it's located in the kidney, he explains. Even papillary cancer—the one Dr. Bukowski still believes Terence had—is so different that few people understand how it behaves. The confusing mass of trial-and-error discovery that I sensed from my forays into the Internet and into the kidney cancer forums was just as real for Dr. Bukowski as it was for us. There was an explosion of research taking place behind the scenes, but nearly all of the new drugs were only known to target the garden-variety clear cell type of cancer that makes up more than 80 percent of the cases.

"You are left with a conundrum," he says. "Do you delay and hope that something will come on the scene? In a patient with a slow-growing cancer, no treatment may be the best treatment."

So *did* Terence have collecting duct cancer?

No, says Dr. Bukowski.

The cancer didn't act like collecting duct, he says. It didn't look like collecting duct. So why did so many expert pathologists think it was?

His answer would sound condescending if the opinion wasn't shared by the pathologists themselves: "A group of leading experts in kidney cancer pathology will not infrequently disagree," he says. He even pulls a card from his sleeve: Back then, he had consulted yet another pathologist at Sloan-Kettering in New York, a leading cancer center, who agreed with Dr. Bukowski that Terence did not have collecting duct.

Dr. Gown in his Seattle pathology lab is unmoved. He looks over his work from 2001 and still concludes he was right. So, I ask Dr. Gown, why didn't Terence's tumor behave like collecting duct? Why did it grow so slowly, when most collecting duct is ferocious in its speed and proliferation?

Dr. Gown shrugs. "Some tumors don't read the book," he says.

So what's the box score on the tumor?

Six pathologists. At least four hospitals. MD Anderson. The Cleveland Clinic. Sloan-Kettering. PhenoPath. Three oncologists. The outcome? Nearly four years after his death, I still don't know what kind of cancer Terence had. Everyone is convinced he is right. Yet, for all our education and experience and the $2.7 billion health care industry that cradles us, we are collectively brought to our knees by Terence's wayward cells.

So why—with all the research I did and the options I found and the insurance payments for drugs I got approved—did Terence and I agree to do nothing?

I'm not sure I know, even today.

I think we trusted Dr. Bukowski. I think that's the reason we did a lot of things we did. For all our research, it wasn't really the science we were following. It was the people. We took the measure of people we trusted and then followed the path they led us on.

14

In the spring of 2003 we are awash in family and friends. My mother and father visit from New Jersey. Georgia's godparents drive up from Atlanta. Terence's old army buddy Woody Boyd comes in from D.C.

And Terence's younger brother roars in from Detroit on his motorcycle.

Younger brother?

A brother for Terence, who grew up in Cincinnati as an only child? Yes, at age sixty-two, Terence is now, much to our surprise, part of a large, far-flung, yet close-knit family. One he didn't even know existed till he was over fifty.

In between our visits to Dr. Bukowski, our life has taken on a pleasingly normal rhythm. Christmas of 2002 comes and goes in our Lexington home. A ceiling-scraping tree sits properly in the front window, its hundreds of lights shining right there for passersby to admire. Most of the 150 people from our newsroom crowd into our house with their families, bearing sugar cookies decorated with Red Hots and tooth-destroying silver pellets, gingerbread men, and rum balls. The copy-desk chief sits at the piano. People sing. Everyone pushes into the living room for his specialty, a hilarious three-minute pastiche of every Christmas carol ever written. On Christmas morning, fourteen-year-old Terry gets a new snare drum and cymbals, Zildjian—the best there is. Georgia, now eight, gets a bike with pink streamers. The world keeps on turning.

As the winter of 2002–2003 edges toward spring, the inexorable post–9/11 march toward Baghdad is picking up steam. No one has found the weapons of mass destruction that they are expecting; everyone keeps asserting they are there. I don't believe it. Terence doesn't believe it. The invasion seems more and more inevitable. Terence is Terence. He flies a flag from our front porch. He reaches out to veterans' groups. He supports my decision to oppose the war. Our paper's editorial board concludes that the evidence does not support an invasion. Don't do it, Mr. President. You have not made your case, we say. We are one of the few papers in the country to write that. My voice mail and email box fill with hateful calls and notes. Other people stop by the building to urge us to do more.

For two weeks in March I sleep in front of the television set. We await the bombing. It will come any day now; if it happens before a certain time, we will stop the presses. When the invasion finally happens, two young men from our staff are there with the troops. One of them, a reporter, is burned by a mysterious chemical. Are these the chemical weapons we are seeking? Another, a photographer, rides into Baghdad in a tank full of soldiers. Every night when I hear from them, I call their moms.

The war wends on. Saddam Hussein's statue is dragged to the ground. There are suicide bombers in Chechnya. Terry learns new Green Day and Blink-182 music. Georgia and her best friend, Bailey, spend most of their waking hours together at Bailey's house, and many nights too. Bailey has a French provincial bedroom, her own bathroom with a large claw-foot tub, and a swimming pool in her backyard. Is it any wonder her home is the playroom of choice? The human genome project is completed. SARS breaks out. Scientists clone a horse, a deer. A gynecologist in a strip mall on the edge of Lexington claims to be cloning a human in an undisclosed European location. We write to debunk his claims. He sues the newspaper.

Terence is teaching and beginning a new project. He wants to start a schoolhouse museum. He prowls the region looking for old schoolhouse items. Our garage swells with initial-carved desks, both tan and dark brown, with hinged lids covering book wells and with cubbies under the seats. He finds fifty-year-old chalkboards, seventy-five-year-old globes. He collects pointers and easels and coal scuttles from one-room schoolhouses. Our cars, once again, are exiled to the driveway. I grouse. When he spots a garage sale Terry and I groan and shout. Only Georgia is enthusiastic. She knows there is costume jewelry in it for her.

It has been nearly fourteen years since Terence and I discovered his lost family. When Terence became a father for the first time at age forty-eight, he began thinking about his own dad, whom he had never met. Increasingly, Terence got an itch to try to find him. In those pre-Internet, pre-Google days, it wasn't all that easy. His mother was dead. The cousins he grew up with are all from her side of the family. They are younger than Terence and they know very little. That left phone books.

Just after Terry's birth in 1988, while we were still living in New York, we spent weekends at the New York Public Library, systematically working through a book at a time, taking the numbers with us to telephone from home.

Whenever we traveled in those days, our first task was to find the phone book and flip to the L's. Nearly a year passed without any luck. Finally my mother, a skilled genealogist, called with a tip, picked up from one of her mysterious sources.

"Try California," she said.

Luckily Terence's dad's name—Laudeman—isn't all that common. There were dozens, not hundreds, to search. Terence began at the north and worked his way down, a couple of names a night, leaving messages or talking to strangers.

Finally, late one night, the phone rang. A wary voice on the other end said he was responding to a message left days earlier. Terence took the phone in the bedroom. He emerged a few minutes later.

"I found him," he said.

As it happened, I was already booked to leave for a business trip to California. We hurriedly bought two more tickets, one for him and one for the year-old Terry. We set off. While I spent days at a conference listening to the drone of economists impressing one another with erudition, Terence took little Terry riding on the cable cars where he once worked. Perhaps they rode the very same cable car! We marveled at the possibility.

When Sunday arrived, we set out driving, following telephoned directions. After about an hour, we pulled into a trailer park.

It is here that I learn how Terence inherited his dramatic flair, and his mania for secrecy. There is the old man, barely five feet five inches tall, standing outside a white double-wide. He is flanked by two middle-aged men wearing blankly wary looks. Just an hour earlier, it turns out, he has summoned the two sons to the house and—just minutes before we arrived—told them his fifty-year-old secret.

"Meet your brother," he says.

If this were a made-for-TV movie, what would happen next? Perhaps a flashback to a romantic scene or two between Terence's parents as teenage lovers. A heartrending moment of anguish with the woman who is now Dad's wife, as she learns the secret for the first time. At the half-hour mark, the younger sons confront their dad. At forty-five minutes Terence and his dad bare their souls to each other, and Terence will confess his pain at his dad's abandonment. By the finale enduring love will triumph over hurt and betrayal.

Nothing remotely like that happens.

We sit through an awkward and strained lunch where we pass

around ancient Polaroids and find out that Terence has not two, but four younger brothers. These four—Fred, Bill, Dick, Charlie—are the children of Myrtle who, for want of a better word, might now be called Terence's stepmother. Although she sits nearly silent through lunch, she seems friendly enough and not at all anxious or edgy. Has she always known the long-buried secret? She claims not, and we never do learn for sure.

Unlike in the made-for-TV-movie version, there are no dramatic professions of love or anger. The Germanic reserve of Terence's Laudeman side triumphs over the untamed volubility of his Foley side. We mince politely around irrelevant subjects and leave.

Still, this is not the end of the story.

Once out of earshot of the parents, the five boys fall on one another with glee, by telephone and later in visits. Whatever the secret or anger or shame of the past, it is immediately clear that no one in this generation shares in it. The four younger boys are as eager to get to know their older brother as Terence is to know them. Cameras. Travel. Motorcycles. Languages. Military service. They compare their life histories and eerily shared memories. They discover that they summered within miles of one another, perhaps even visiting the same Cincinnati-area relatives on the same weeks, or even days, but never encountering one another.

By the end of a week, they are Uncle Fred. Uncle Charlie. Uncle Bill. Uncle Dick. We like one another. We visit one another's homes. Get to know one another's children. Little Terry is suddenly one of fourteen half cousins. On my bedroom wall a photo still hangs from the wedding of Fred's oldest son. There gathered together are the lost siblings, in one place for the first—and as it turns out, last—time. There they stand in a row, sturdy, barrel-chested German stalwarts all, each of the six of them round-faced, stout, and open.

Six? Yes, six. For that is the biggest surprise of all. For in addition to the four boys, it turns out there is another child, a girl, from yet a third wife in the old man's past.

This lost girl, now a grown woman with seven children of her own, is—for me—the missing piece in Terence's family story that never quite added up otherwise. Why did Terence's dad leave the scene so suddenly? Why did he leave behind a pregnant wife and never look back? Why were there no cards? No letters? No visits? Even though, as we discover fifty years later, the families are regularly crossing paths?

Terence grew up hearing his mother, Ruth, tell a whimsical story that to my ears never quite rang true. In this version, she and his father, Turner—sweethearts since high school, and married for seven years after—amicably agree to divorce but only on Ruth's giggling condition: that she become pregnant first. That mission accomplished, she lets him go and never sees him again.

Does this make sense? Does this explain the total estrangement? The fact that the father never seeks out his son? The mother never introduces the father? The brothers who pass yearly at the farm in Ohio and share visits with the same relatives never meet?

Not to me.

Nothing explains that estrangement to my satisfaction until I meet Terence's sister. In our excited conversations with our new relatives we compare biographical details. All at once the mathematics of the past's secrets leap out. Terence, the eldest of the old man's children, is born to Ruth on September 4, 1940. And when is Terence's open-faced younger sister Artie born to Virginia, Turner's second wife?

January 20, 1941, just four and a half months later. Did a hurtful infidelity cause the rift? Did Turner really know Ruth was pregnant? Did Ruth know that Virginia was? Is Artie even Turner's child at all?

Everyone who knows the true story is dead.

15

In the slow summery days of 2003, we increasingly feel that Lexington is our home. We may live here forever, we think.

On South Ashland Avenue the bulbs we planted the previous fall bloom and die—jonquils in the front, hyacinths in the back. We go to the Kentucky Derby. I buy a huge floppy white hat with a purple peony. Terence wears blue seersucker and a boater. We win a hundred dollars. We lose a hundred dollars. We drink mint juleps and sing "My Old Kentucky Home." Funny Cide takes the prize, the first gelding to win since 1929, which yields predictable wisecracks. I play practical jokes on my boss; he stings one back at me. His wife, a nurse, keeps tabs on us.

And then, all of a sudden, it is time to move.

In late spring, I travel with all the other Knight Ridder editors to our annual gathering in California. We trade notes, compare experiences, sit through long PowerPoint sessions on the company's finances. At dinner the night I return, I regale the children with the pranks that even grown-ups like to play—including a caper in which all of us editors band together to steal as many household items as we can out from under the nose of our host.

The children are enchanted.

After they leave for bed, I casually continue the conversation with Terence.

"Does Tony Ridder know you?" I ask, referring to the chairman of the company I work for that bears his name.

"No, not at all," Terence says. "Why?"

"He was very interested in what you are doing, asking lots of questions," I say. At the cocktail party, Tony did in fact seem very interested in Terence. What does he do? How long has he done it? How does he like Lexington?

Terence's face lights up.

"We're moving!" he says.

"Huh?"

"We're moving," says Terence. "It's obvious."

"You're crazy," I say. "He was just being polite."

"Not a chance," he says. "They've got a big job for you. We're moving."

"We're not moving again!" I say. "We just got here. I like it here."

The next morning when I leave for work, Terence is already in the basement, inventorying boxes.

"You're out of your mind," I say. "Have fun!"

Shortly after lunch, my boss calls me into his office.

Philadelphia!

I am not sure what I am expecting, but certainly not the monumental view that greets me as I step out of my hotel on my first day in Philadelphia. The Benjamin Franklin Parkway. The starkly classical Free Library and Family Court buildings. The reddish brick Italian Renaissance Cathedral Basilica of Saints Peter and Paul. The Franklin Institute. The Rodin Museum. The Swann Fountain with its Native American figures. And off in the distance to the left, looking like the Acropolis, the Philadelphia Museum of Art hulking over the whole scene. To the right, City Hall with its fussy detail and its statue of William Penn atop the clock tower. Soon enough the children will discover the hilarious—to a fourteen-year-old and a nine-year-old—phallic view that can be had of Old Billy if you stand and look at him from a certain angle.

Everything about Philadelphia seems monumental. Its buildings. Its history. Its art. Its poverty. Its sheer daunting size—143 square miles that stretch out far beyond any place any visitor normally ventures. Even *The Philadelphia Inquirer*—Knight Ridder's flagship paper—is monumental. The paper's square-shouldered white building topped by a clock tower and dome can be clearly seen from miles away. The top story is the former home of Walter Annenberg, the paper's onetime publisher.

And the newsroom! The newsroom! It too is monumental, like no other newsroom in America. It is like everyone's fantasy of a newsroom—only more so. In perhaps one of the most improbably thoughtful acts of industrial redesign, the newsroom has been carved out of the space that the paper's presses once occupied. The news floor is as long as a football field, and its ceiling soars the equivalent of four stories up. The entire whitewashed space is punctuated by massive white columns, while a balcony that rings the room is big enough to house a quarter of the paper's five-hundred-plus reporters and editors and photographers. The walk into the newsroom is a daunting one, past framed certificates of the paper's Pulitzer Prizes—eighteen of them over the previous eighty-six years.

The newsroom is particularly daunting for me. The paper is teetering on the edge of the disaster that will engulf all newspapers all too soon as readers and advertisers flee to the Internet. I know I am the first woman editor in the paper's 174-year history. It's in all the news stories. Yet I don't fully realize what that means until I take stock of the newsroom on my first day at work. The entire place is a hearty, overexaggerated paean to maleness, from the brooding nineteenth-century-style editor's office that looks straight out of Dickens—oversized mahogany credenza, dark walnut paneling, and stand-up desk—to the trophies of past editors' athletic pursuits. The crossed oars of one—a rower—dominates one end of the newsroom, flanked by the hockey jerseys of another. Framed overwrought tributes from one past male editor to another dot the room.

Others apparently have noticed too. When I arrive that morning, I find a gigantic pink girdle suspended across the front of my office. It is a reference to a wiseguy remark I make in my opening speech about relaxing and taking it easy in our jobs. There is a sign attached: Welcome Amanda Bennett, First Woman Editor. It is an affectionate and hopeful sign.

I think.

We throw ourselves into the city. We force the grousing children—by now at ages fourteen and nine just a touch too old for this—into field trips. Independence Hall. Carpenters' Hall. Valley Forge. We walk on streets still covered in cobblestones. "Benjamin Franklin probably walked here," we tell them. "George Washington probably sat here." Philadelphia has become a mecca for chic and edgy food. Le Bec-Fin is called America's finest French restaurant. All around it, new restaurants sprout up. Stephen Starr opens the sexy Striped Bass. El Vez. Buddakan. The futuristic Pod. The city also spews trendy BYOs that you need to reserve three months in advance.

That's not where we go. Instead Terence prowls the narrow streets of South Philly, with their white-sided rowhouses, narrow front porches, green aluminum awnings, and front windows that flaunt decorations for every holiday. He finds the old Philly red gravy joints and we drag the kids out every Friday night for spaghetti and meatballs or ziti with big, fat sausages in thick red sauce. Criniti's. Dante & Luigi's. Tre Scalini. Ralph's. Vesuvio. Before a month is out we have sampled every cheesesteak. Pat's.

Geno's. Jim's on South Street. John's Roast Pork on Snyder. Terence finds the bakeries (Termini Brothers, Isgro) and the best cheese shop in the Italian market (Di Bruno Brothers). He learns to make pasta e fagioli and Italian wedding soup. We find a Quaker school for the children—ninth grade for Terry, fourth grade for Georgia—just a few blocks from my new office.

And so we settle in to what will be our last home together.

This is Philly, so we buy a Philly house, a tall, narrow brick rowhouse with red shutters and a basement door that slants from the house to the sidewalk. It was built in 1850. It is being used as an apartment building. We rip out the insides and turn it back into a home. I would be happy living with the chairs I bought from Goodwill when I was in college; with the coffee table made from a giant discarded wooden spool used for electrical cables; with the old church pew I bought when a Methodist church in Toronto was hollowed out to make room for a Hare Krishna enclave.

It is only because of Terence that we live like grown-ups. Over the years he makes us buy proper wing chairs. Antique rugs: two from China, one from India, one from Pakistan. A mahogany china cabinet. A grandfather clock. Floor-to-ceiling white bookshelves filled with novels and plays and poetry, with vases and family photos. He hangs oil paintings and sketches he has bought all over Asia. A still-faced Vietnamese girl, her hands folded quietly in her lap, looks hauntingly down on our dining table.

Time has softened us both.

Yet we still lock horns in angry arguments, usually when he refuses to do something exactly the way I want, or I refuse to do something exactly the way he wants. I explode at the sight of him sitting in the living room chair, hat and coat on and car keys in his hand as I try to get a teen, a preteen, and me out the door in the morning. There is lunch money to dole out, shoes to be found, lost homework papers, breakfast to be levered in. Why won't he help? There is so much to do!

He won't budge.

"You think you can leave at eight and get there by seven thirty," he says, not stirring from the chair. "You always have."

I crab and rant. Why do you always...? Why don't you ever...? Why are you so...? We trade mindless barbs. After we drop the kids off, I fling the car door shut and stomp off to work. A half hour later, I see his cell number pop up.

I snarl at the ringing office phone: "I'm not answering. I'm still mad. You can just forget it. I'm not speaking to you."

I pick up the receiver.

I hear him say: "I'm sorry..."

Then there is a long pause.

"...that you are such an asshole."

I laugh. I can't help myself.

Then comes another day, and another meaningless fight. What is it about? I no longer have any idea. Afterward, I drive myself to work, talking to myself all the way, replaying the argument, winning this time. Thinking of the words that will once and for all prove me right and him wrong. Chewing out the phone for daring to ring, even as I bring the receiver to my ear.

"All right! All right!" he growls. "I accept your damned apology."

My assistant pokes her head in the door to see why I am laughing so hard.

Over dinner one night, I tell the children about how, years earlier, Terence and I watched a dramatic helicopter rescue of an injured skier in Glacier National Park. "That was the day Daddy locked the keys in the car," I say.

"Mommy," Terence says.

"Mommy what?" I ask.

"The day *Mommy* locked the keys in the car."

"Daddy," I say.

"Mommy," he repeats.

Terry slaps his hand on the table.

"WHO locked the keys in the car?"

"Daddy."

"Mommy."

Georgia kicks the table.

"WHO locked the keys in the car?"

"Daddy."

"Mommy."

Each time we revisit the story it is the same. Each time the children demand to know the truth. They stamp their feet. Who did it? Who locked the keys in the car?

Daddy.

Mommy.

Terence is long gone, and Terry is well past drinking age when something dawns on him.

"I was so mad at both of you. I thought you were messing with us because we were kids," he says. "I just realized now that you both actually BELIEVED it."

"It was Daddy," I say.

Meanwhile, just because we aren't doing anything to treat the cancer doesn't mean we aren't doing anything at all. Every three or four months we return to the Cleveland Clinic to see Dr. Bukowski and to make sure that the cancer is keeping quiet. While we live in Lexington we drive there. When we move to Philly, he flies. The medical records that I collect after his death give a stark, professional account of these punctuation marks in our lives.

July 21, 2003: Stable. November 10, 2003: Stable. March 11, 2004: Stable. August 30, 2004: Stable; see him in three months. January 31, 2005: Stable. March 21, 2005: Stable.

At each visit, Dr. Bukowski orders tests that will let us see what the cancer is up to. Sometimes there are whole body scans. Sometimes there are scans of his abdomen, or his lungs. There are blood tests and X-rays. Every three or four months we hold our breath while we wait for the news. Every three or four months we exhale when the news is good.

As I look back over the medical records from that time, I see that we are billed at least $4,500 for each trip to the Cleveland Clinic, including separate bills for scans, for Dr. Bukowski, and for the doctors who, behind the scenes, read the scans. The bills for our November 10 visit, copied from our UnitedHealthcare insurance statement, go like this:

$2,819 Cleveland Clinic
$1,449 CAT scans
$118 Dr. Bukowski
$318 Dr. Barbara Risius
$280 Dr. Brian Herts
$329 Dr. Brian Herts

Three years, eight visits, from $4,500 to more than $5,300 each. That's more than $36,000 during a time when we are simply watching and waiting. I do not realize this until I look over the records, and I am sure Terence never does know. How do we spend $36,000 without thinking about it?

I am flustered and disorganized with bills, but I am a pretty good shopper. So is Terence. He grew up with lace tablecloths and fresh flowers and his mother's twelve-place silver set that I use today and will someday give to Georgia. I grew up with secondhand furniture, buying groceries on credit at the neighborhood store, and going with my mother twice a week to the Laundromat on the hill with the family's washing. Yet we both arrive at the same place: Both of us buy sensible things at good prices after serious consideration. Yet we rack up $36,000 in charges without a thought.

When I shop for groceries I check my receipt to see if the two-for-one ShopRite special on yogurt has registered. Terence buys huge boxes of cereal at Sam's Club. We shop carefully for shoes, for tires, for lightbulbs, lawn mowers, and toothpaste. It never occurs to us to shop for CAT scans.

Month in and month out, despite the reassuring news, it remains hard to do nothing when I have promised myself to do everything I can. So I do my best to keep the other half of the promise I made on that dark night in Lexington.

Every night as we sit down to dinner—the proper dinner he insists on with place mats and napkins and serving dishes, forks on the left, knives and spoons on the right—we hold hands and thank God that we are all together again. Every day, at least once a day—by cellphone, by email, in person, at breakfast, or just before bed—I tell Terence how much he means to me. How much he means to our family. How much I see and appreciate everything he does for us. I tell him how funny he is, and how smart. I tell him what a good dad he is, and what a good friend.

And every single day, I tell him just how much I love him.

And so we continue until December 19, 2005. Six days before Christmas, Terence returns from his visit with Dr. Bukowski with the news that his cancer has begun to grow again, and our long wait is over.

16

On December 19, 2005, everything changes.

From this moment on, the rhythms of our weeks will be punctuated by the pace of a clinical trial of an experimental cancer drug. We join forces with a doctor who is staking his whole life on believing that everything in the cancer world is about to be transformed, and that this drug is only the beginning.

After that, the days of our lives together are guided by Dr. Keith Flaherty—a doctor we have just met—and girded by sorafenib, a drug whose name neither Terence nor I can spell, and bevacizumab, a drug whose name neither of us can pronounce. Our calendar is linked with the calendar of the trial and our emotional ease rises and falls with the timing of the monthly scans that accompany the treatment.

Yet in many ways, nothing changes at all.

Today, as I review the records and the research, the stark reality of even the most optimistic outcome leaps out at me. Even the best chances were slim, I can see in retrospect. Yet back then, hard as I looked, I saw none of that. Terence and I believe in these drugs with a belief that is beyond belief. Partly as a result of our belief, for the next year and a half, these drugs buy us a normal life.

They buy us hope.

Our life is so normal, in fact, that I have trouble recalling much of what happened during this time. Yet today, to jog my memory of the sheer ordinariness of our days, I have only to pop into the

VCR one of the dozens of home videos Terence created. On March 26, 2010, two years, three months, and twelve days after his death, I summon the courage to pull a few home videos from the family room shelf, searching for the clues to help me remember.

On the tapes, hours and hours and hours of images unfold, scenes from our lives here in Philadelphia. Girls sit at the kitchen counter on high-backed chairs—Georgia, and her friends Alex, Taylor, Kaitlyn, all smiles and giggles. Our flower boxes fill and empty and then fill again. The flag goes up and the flag comes down. In Halloween costumes, Terry, Isaac, Ben, Maddy, Nico, and Suzie mug for the camera. Georgia shows off a school project. Terry steals a hug with Suzie. "Go away!" he shouts over his shoulder at the camera.

Georgia has a birthday party—perhaps my single proudest "good mom" moment. At our local discount store, I buy cases of chocolate syrup and whipped cream, and I stay up late making vats of Jell-O. Then I put the girls into bathing suits and turn them loose on one another. I hear Terence behind the camera warning the shrieking and sticky would-be attackers away from him as ropes of chocolate and chunks of Jell-O fly through the air.

Our house fills with friends. They make coffee in our kitchen. They twirl pasta. They drink wine and talk. Everywhere, there is food. Crumb cakes. Upside-down cakes. Party treats cover the tables. Pots simmer on the stove. Terence and I both wear aprons.

In one Christmas shot, we torment the children as they loop silver strands through the branches of the tree.

"Christmas in our new house!" I cry. "Where will we be next year?"

"Not next year," Terence replies. "TWO more Christmases in this house. THEN we move."

The children ignore us. I cover them with Christmas kisses. Then I vanish off the screen. "And here's a kiss for the camera-man," I hear myself saying. In the background, I hear a brass quintet play "Joy to the World," the minor chords and major chords interchanging seamlessly, the darkness and the light weaving in and out.

The dailiness of our lives.

That is what hope buys us.

17

The last report we get from the Cleveland Clinic on December 19, 2005, doesn't sound all that ominous to us.

Terence has gone there as usual for his quarterly checkup and scan. All the report says is that the scan shows "further progression of a right upper lobe mass, but stability in numerous small lung lesions." It sounds okay to me and to Terence, different certainly, but not that much different from any of the other reports we have received over the past four years.

But Dr. Bukowski sees something else. The cancer, indolent, sluggish, and lazy up till now, has begun to grow again. That is enough for Dr. Bukowski. With the same certainty with which he told us in 2002 to wait and do nothing, he now galvanizes us to action. Perhaps it is now time to investigate something more aggressive—some clinical trials and treatments closer to home. He tells us about Dr. Flaherty, who is beginning a promising study in Philadelphia. Our next stop, Dr. Bukowski tells us, should be Presbyterian Hospital, where Dr. Flaherty will explain to us what he hopes the clinical trial he is conducting will achieve.

Joining a clinical trial has been a focus of our obsession right from the beginning of Terence's illness. For a cancer like his—with no really effective known treatment—it's the only hope for most people. You can enter the lottery using the known treatments, as

Terence and Dr. Pierce secretly did, and take the chance that you will be one of the lucky ones mysteriously helped. Or—if that fails—you can enter a clinical trial. That's a lottery with even longer odds. Yet this is perhaps part of the reason lotteries and horse racing and Internet gambling have such appeal. The promise of the big payoff overwhelms our judgment about our slim chances. Why shouldn't we be the smart ones? Why shouldn't we be the lucky ones? Why shouldn't we push the bell curve? Why shouldn't we escape fate?

To dive into the world of trials, though, is to dive into a pool writhing with serpents looking for diamonds. On Monday, April 25, 2011, ClinicalTrials.gov, the National Institutes of Health database of all such trials, lists 106,373 trials in 174 countries. There are 1,641 of them involving kidney cancer—and 678 of those are recruiting new subjects. That's the same order of magnitude I remember from the years Terence and I were looking. There were—and still are—hundreds and hundreds and hundreds of trials, and no clear way of deciding which one to choose.

Long before we even found Dr. Bukowski, we began our search for clinical trials that might help Terence. Much of the chatter on the kidney cancer listserv back in 2001, 2002, and 2003 involved finding, evaluating, and handicapping the various clinical trials and trading information about the doctors running them. It was information about clinical trials that I clutched when I met Dr. Pierce, and he politely considered and followed up. It was sheets on clinical trials that I thrust at Dr. Bukowski at our first meeting and that he resolutely ignored.

So what did we consider over the years? On a white lined pad I recorded notes of the trials we were investigating. I scribbled place names: Memorial Sloan-Kettering. MD Anderson.

Roswell Park Cancer Institute. Where is that? Buffalo. Buffalo?

Fox Chase in Pennsylvania, from long before we have any idea where Fox Chase—a suburb of Philadelphia—even is. The University of Alabama and University of California, San Francisco. Even one in Nebraska. Nebraska??

My notes show that the range of options we considered is staggering. Nonmyeloablative bone marrow transplant. I can't even remember what that means anymore. I have to Google it: It's a method of transplanting donor bone marrow cells that isn't as toxic or dangerous to the patient as traditional ways. That part sounded good. But whose cells? His only blood relatives are his cousins and his newfound half siblings. We imagined the conversation: Hi there! We haven't spoken for the past fifty years. Welcome to our lives. Can we have some stem cells? We did some more research. It didn't sound promising enough to cross that bridge.

On the pad is a note to myself: "Chemo and irradiation. It improves the graft vs. tumor effect (check this) and the immune response to the tumor." From the listserv we learned that Janice Dutcher—at Our Lady of Mercy Medical Center in the Bronx—was doing a trial of ABX-Epigenics. What's that? Does the listserv even have that right? There was one trial of Iressa at Vanderbilt and another trial of thalidomide, the antinausea drug that created babies with flippers instead of arms and legs, being tested in combination with interferon. Fox Chase is doing CCI-779. Virginia Mason is doing Gleevec. Cleveland Clinic has a trial of Neovastat, made from shark's cartilage. There's one vaccine trial, and at MD Anderson a trial of SU5416, which inhibits the VEGF receptor. The names, places, drugs, concepts are dizzying. How do we choose? Whom do we trust?

I was obviously reaching for anything, and taking it seriously. In my notes, I see a confirmation number for MD Anderson—051102162016FIK—and a registration for an appointment for a scan in the hospital in Houston. There were the names of the nurse-practitioners all across the country—the only people who actually take the time to talk with us about our options: Ann. Blanca. Julie. Jacqueline. Noel.

There were so many things to think about it made our heads hurt. The point of a clinical trial is to test—in people—how different drugs work. The trials aren't designed for patients. They're designed for science. Each design differs depending on the type of drug and the knowledge that the researcher is seeking. Some are logistically difficult. One—in a faraway state—required daily injections in a hospital for thirty days. We would have had to move there for at least a month. What about the children? Unless we thought this was a sure bet, that one seemed out. Some of them were testing a new drug against nothing at all. We didn't want to do that. After all, if there was a chance that half of the participants were going to—without knowing it—get only a placebo, then that meant our already slim chances would be cut in half. Some of the studies were testing new drugs against the existing standard of care. One of these compared a new drug combination with interleukin-2. That meant there was a 50–50 chance Terence would wind up with another round of the IL-2 that made him so miserable in Lexington. No way we were going back to that.

Some of the trials—a lot of them, in fact—specifically excluded the odd cancers like papillary and collecting duct. Once we read deeply into the rules of some intriguing trials, we realized that the researchers were limiting their subjects to those 80 percent who had the common clear cell variety. Some of the trials—like ones for a vegan diet or for laetrile—appeared to be designed simply to rule out treatments that patients demand but that doctors didn't think hold promise. And some, I learn much later, after Terence's death, were known informally and privately as "throw the spaghetti against the wall" trials. During these years, a dawning recognition that the place of origin of a cancer—bladder, kidney, breast, colon—might be less important than the cancer's genetic composition led researchers on flights of possibilities. If a drug worked against colon cancer, let's try it for breast cancer. If it worked for breast cancer, let's try it for kidney cancer. That, weirdly enough, turns out to be one of the best options, for it was that almost random testing that led the doctor in Paris—almost accidentally—to discover how well the drug that would become Sutent worked on kidney cancer.

So how to put ourselves where this kind of lightning will strike? How would we find out which trials were serious? Which kinds were duds? In which trials were patients seeming to recover? In which ones was nothing happening?

I remember Laura Lear, who posted as lmodrngrrl. The last post of hers that I read was very hopeful. She had gotten her boyfriend, Robert Cowen, the experimental drug Gleevec. His collecting duct kidney tumors were shrinking. He was feeling better. I hadn't checked back on them since December 2002. How are they doing?

I searched out her name on the listserv. I saw his name and two dates in the subject line: Robert Cowen: October 26, 1959–September 9, 2003. I snapped the computer off and didn't return to our search for several days.

So how did we eventually choose? How did we figure out which ones would work for us and which ones wouldn't? We never really did. My notes show lists of phone numbers. Trial administrators. Doctors. Even drug company scientific representatives. Talking to them about the trials was tough. Officially they weren't supposed to try to stack the deck, say, by encouraging people to join who look like they might benefit from the treatment—which is just what I wanted them to do. The needs of science came smack up against Terence's and my needs. If it seemed the trial would benefit us, we would be more likely to join, and the results of the trial would perhaps look better than they should. That's why so many of my questions along the way to the testers hit a brick wall.

So is this going to WORK? I demanded of each investigator, knowing full well the lunacy of the question. If they knew it would work, why would they conduct a·trial? What I was really asking was: Does this have a chance? Does it make sense for us? Out of the hundreds of possibilities, why would we pick this one? Most of my queries were met with a polite official nonanswer and a faxed sheet of the study's requirements. Quietly, though, every so often someone would nudge with just enough information to intrigue us.

In the end, one of the reasons we agreed so readily with Dr. Bukowski's assessment that the best thing we could do was nothing is that we never did find anything—up to that point—that we thought seriously competed for our attention.

Behind the scenes, I learn many years later, horse trading does go on. Doctors know what their colleagues are up to; they know which trials are doing well and which are duds. When they have patients they think might benefit, they can steer them to the right place.

Of course, on the other hand, I find out years later that—just as we suspect—there is also huge pressure to recruit patients into one's own clinical trial. And why wouldn't there be? Clinical trials are a big business. They mean money for the institutions. Money for the doctors. Professional citations on research papers for the assistants. Professional advancement for the lead investigators. Not to mention the possibility of fame if the experiment succeeds.

Everyone along our journey seemed to be totally committed to their chosen role as healers. We thought they were good people. We trusted them. Yet it was impossible not to feel all those outside pressures as well.

Several years into our relationship with Dr. Bukowski, just such pressures crack—just a tiny bit—our feeling of solidarity with this man we have come to trust. At one of our regular meetings

with him in Cleveland, on March 21, 2005, he asks us to partici-
pate in a clinical trial that he is conducting.

He leaves the room. A nurse, Sharon O'Keefe, enters with a
consent form describing the trial:

> *An Ascending Single and Multiple Dose Study of the Safety,*
> *Tolerability Pharmacokinetics and Pharmacodynamics of HKI-272*
> *Administered Orally to Subjects with HER2/neu or HER-1/EGFR-*
> *Positive Tumors*

The drug is owned by Wyeth Research. Dr. Bukowski is listed
as investigator. The topic is familiar. *HER2/neu* is a gene found in
excess in aggressive breast cancers. Herceptin, a relatively new
drug at the time, is being used to treat certain kinds of breast
cancer. We know from earlier tests that Terence's tumor, like
many other kidney cancers, also shows signs of the *HER2/neu*
gene. I even earlier got Terence approved to use a breast-cancer
drug that worked against this gene. We begin to read the document. We are excited by what we read. The drug attacks this exact
situation.

> *HKI-272 is an experimental drug. In laboratory studies, HKI–272*
> *stopped cancer cells from growing by attaching itself to proteins*
> *called HER-2 and HER-1 which are members of a family of*
> *receptors found on both cancer and normal cells.*

So far so good. Then, suddenly, our eyes meet. We have come
to the same spot in the document . . . paragraphs four and five.

> *This is a Phase I trial of the experimental drug HKI-272 . . .*
> *   It is emphasized that the goal of a Phase I study is to measure*
> *toxicity, not response of your tumor. The primary objective is to find*
> *the maximally tolerated dose of the new drug.*

A phase I trial? Measure toxicity? We read on. Each patient will take the drug at a different dose, to measure when the side effects become intolerable. Six cycles of the drug. Twenty visits to the Cleveland Clinic during the test—for blood tests, eye exams, questions about side effects, electrocardiograms, physical exams.

We read further. On page 6, the possible side effects are described: blood in the urine, decreased or no feces, hair loss, increased white blood cells, and lesions around the nose and/or mouth, diarrhea, nausea, vomiting, weakness, fatigue, fever, chills, headache, difficulty breathing... The list goes on and on.

Terence can barely stand the side effects of IL-2 when he thinks there is a chance it can help him. We are stunned. Inside the examining room we say nothing. Outside, we confer.

"I don't want to just be a guinea pig, goddammit," Terence shouts, once safely in the car. "I want to get better."

The clinic record for that day is terse:

Mar. 21—clinical presentation of study. KIRBY #6631 on HKI-272 for subjects with HER2/neu or HER-1/EGFR positive tumors. Reviewed with patient and wife. Financial responsibilities regarding procedures and medications discussed. Patient given copy of consent. Signed by Sharon O'Keefe, RN.

The United Healthcare record shows the clinic bills $138 for the visit. The records from Terence's last meeting with Dr. Bukowski on December 19, 2005, simply note that since Terence has refused clinical trials at the Cleveland Clinic, the "best option" is to try one of the other trials.

Dr. Bukowski knows we are looking for treatment. He knows that we want to prolong Terence's life. So why does he offer this trial?

In 2009, when I fly to Cleveland to meet the now-retired Dr. Bukowski at the clinic, I ask him just that question. Given that we had been coming to you looking to extend Terence's life, why would you offer us a trial of a drug that would benefit the drug maker, maybe the hospital, possibly you, and—possibly—patients in the future, but not Terence himself?

"Because he was eligible for it," says Dr. Bukowski.

That's all he says. The conversation moves on. We turn to other subjects, but I am still not satisfied. At the end of the interview, I ask again. It's one of the few really sore spots in our saga. I want to make sure that I know what he is thinking.

Why did you offer us this trial of something that wouldn't help him? I ask again. I really want to know. I know Terence did too.

Because he was eligible for it, he says again.

Because he was eligible for it.

The trial he steers us to in January 2006 is different, though, almost the mirror image of the one we rejected in March 2005. This new one is a test of two compounds that are both known to be effective against kidney cancer. This trial will test whether the two drugs work better together than each does alone.

We jump at it.

18

From a distance, down the halls of Presbyterian Hospital in Philadelphia in January 2006, Dr. Keith Flaherty looks much bigger—and older—than he actually is. When he draws near we can see that he is not tall—a little more than midway between my five feet two inches and Terence's five feet ten. From a distance his premature baldness gives him a dignified and statesmanlike air. When he comes closer we can see that he is considerably younger than either of us. We will later learn he is just thirty-five years old when we first meet him. When we ask him questions, he prefaces his answers with long pauses. At first we think he hasn't heard, or is distracted, but we come to realize he is just framing careful answers.

When he talks, he gives the impression of having all the time in the world for us, something I later discover has been his hallmark ever since his student days. While Terence furiously scribbles on his index cards, Dr. Flaherty lays out the logic of the clinical trial Terence is about to join. Nexavar—also called sorafenib—is the first new drug to treat kidney cancer in more than a decade. On December 20, 2005, less than a month before our meeting with Dr. Flaherty, Nexavar was approved by the FDA after tests showed that it more than doubled the survival rate of those taking it. The co-lead investigator on that study, I will later learn: Dr. Bukowski.

So who is this Dr. Flaherty? More than two years after Terence's death, a colleague, Ken Wells, and I spend hours visiting

with him. Why kidney cancer? Why cancer at all? When he graduated from Yale in 1993 he thought of Wall Street. "I saw money
for the sake of money and I saw medicine," he says. "And I wasn't
sure which one I wanted." The choice probably wasn't really as
hard as he makes it out to be: He's the third child of two doctors—
a psychiatrist and a cardiologist—the grandchild of another, and
the spouse of yet another.

In medical school, what experience did he seek out? "I was focused on trying to find intensity and drama. I wasn't trying to shy
away, to go into ophthalmology or plastic surgery or some other
boutique-ish profession that was about billing instead of illness. I
wanted to take care of people who were ill or who were desperately afraid that they were."

And when he got to the University of Pennsylvania hospital in
2002, what kind of cancer was he drawn to? "To be a renal cell
specialist ten years ago was pretty grim," he says. The only treatment available was the IL-2 that made Terence so ill in Lexington. Specialists at the hospital grouped cancers by their location,
so one practice focused on kidney, bladder, testes, and prostate
cancer. Of those, kidney cancer was the "least favorite" of one of
his colleagues, because there was no hope. "My colleague was
thrilled to give that to me: 'Please, you deal with this. I don't want
it, thank you very much.'"

He began to work with new drugs. The kinds of drugs he now
offers to Terence—drugs that attack the blood supply of the
tumor, drugs that find the individual chemical signature that
makes cells grow out of control. Drugs that target special pathways. He treated, he says, "if not the first, then the second" kidney
cancer patient with Nexavar. He and a colleague in Chicago
latched onto a "spaghetti against the wall" trial and tried Nexavar
out on one patient each. "We said, 'This is a drug that could work
here.' And sure enough, it did."

To Dr. Flaherty, the shadows that Terence and I have chased

for years weren't shadows at all, but real colleagues and real trials. Before long, he and his Chicago colleague were treating 210 people in five places with Nexavar. "We just went kind of hog wild," Dr. Flaherty says. Meanwhile, behind the scenes, others were testing what would later become Sutent.

"I call [a colleague] and say, 'Bob, what have you got? Is there something that's looking promising, something worth this patient making the trip up there once a month to be in a trial up there?' We were perfectly honest about that. It's clinical trials, but it's really patient care. It's not top secret stuff. It's people with cancer we're trying to help."

He and others begin to realize that not just one, but many of these drugs were beginning to help people. "That was an exciting time: There are relatively few moments in medicine when you get the chill-up-the-spine kind of feeling—so much of what we do is a gradual day-by-day patient-by-patient process. This was a major leap forward."

Cancer doctors do burn out, he says. All those funerals. All those grieving relatives.

It is the discovery that makes it all worthwhile.

"Burning out on this would be like burning out on life," he says.

Dr. Flaherty has two young children and a weekend house in the Pennsylvania woods. He collects American first editions—a copy of *V* by Thomas Pynchon, a manuscript copy of *Infinite Jest*. He listens to Springsteen. Like Terence, he wears bow ties. Like Terence, he reads poetry. On his nightstand is Marvin Bell, an American poet most famous for his works "The Dead Man" and "The Dead Man Speaks."

"The dead man is the only one who will live forever," reads one of Bell's poems.

Dr. Flaherty and Terence talk for hours about cancer. About the treatments. About cells and chemistry and the trials. Terence scribbles, scribbles, scribbles on his index cards.

"He had a very intellectual approach to his illness," says Dr. Flaherty.

Nexavar, like many of the new drugs that were then still on the horizon, treats cancer by interrupting its ability to grow blood vessels to feed itself. Like an alien army marching across a fertile new territory, cancer builds supply chains to provide the nutrients to keep itself growing. Nexavar chokes off those supply chains. Without a way to tap into the bloodstream for food, the cancer withers and dies.

Avastin—bevacizumab—won't be approved by the FDA to treat kidney cancer until August 2009, more than a year and a half after Terence's death. But by the time we join the study, it is already clear that it too is effective against the cancer's blood-building pathways.

Dr. Flaherty explains the study's rules: A tablet of Nexavar by mouth every day. An hour-long Avastin drip at the hospital every two weeks. Every month, a CAT scan of his chest to check on the size of the metastases. Terence and I are both eager to start. Dr. Flaherty's notes from our first visit reflect this: Mr. Foley "expressed a strong interest in pursuing" the combination. "It will be several weeks before he can go on study, but the pace of disease continues to be slow and I think that this does not pose a risk to him." United Healthcare pays $53.55 of the $118 charge for the visit. I don't remember who paid the rest, but it must have been me.

We begin the trial at the end of February 2006.

We pick the Nexavar up at the pharmacy inside our Superfresh grocery store. Gino, the pharmacist, has to special order it. It's not something he keeps on hand. Terence takes one tablet every day,

400 milligrams of the drug. Once a week, Terence drives across town from our rowhouse on the east side of Philadelphia and across the Schuylkill River to Presbyterian Hospital, a part of the University of Pennsylvania, on the west side of the city, where he sits and reads for an hour while he gets his Avastin drip. On March 28, 2006, he finishes his first four-week cycle and has his first CAT scans to see the results. Nothing much has changed.

Another month. Another cycle. Another CAT scan. Same results. At least the tumors aren't growing anymore, we think. But by June 2006, the fourth month of the trial, the scans have a new story to tell. Not only are there no new lesions in his lungs, the biggest of the original ones have begun to shrink. They are so much smaller, in fact, that Dr. Flaherty's notes pronounce Terence a confirmed "partial response"—meaning that the metastases are now at least a third smaller than they were when we began.

The Avastin/Nexavar combination is working. We have dodged the bullet once again. It never occurs to me to think: Just how long will this work? It is working. That is enough for me.

And so our life resumes a normal rhythm. I drive the kids to school. Terence picks them up. Terry goes to rock school, where he learns to play Radiohead. The Grateful Dead. Queen. Frank Zappa. Georgia turns twelve and heads off to summer camp. Together we sew a blue flowered dress for the end-of-camp dance. Terry is seventeen and heading into his senior year in high school. Terence continues teaching journalism classes at Temple University and Drexel University.

In between teaching and Avastin drips, he packs boxes for the troops in battle, loading them in our kitchen with deodorant, wet wipes, Mars bars, Kool-Aid, beef jerky, batteries, and magazines. This veteran of naval intelligence and the air force reserves walks almost every day the four blocks to the post office on Fourth

Street with a box addressed to "Any Soldier." Behind the counter, Deborah, the smiling lady with the long red hair extensions, becomes his friend. Every so often a soldier in Iraq or Afghanistan drops him a thank-you note.

Meanwhile, our cache of cats has increased to four. Finally, after many tries, we find a cat who loves Terence as much as Terence loves him. The tiny male tiger I rescued from drowning at a Lexington horse farm has grown into a majestic beast. Terence names him Hank. Yet the children and I still recall him as a ferocious six-week-old kitten with the genes of his barn-cat parents. He terrorized the older cats, whacking them across the nose with his tiny paws and roaring across the room straight up the drapes, where he had to be rescued from the top. Georgia and Terry and I call him LT—short for "Little Terror."

Even after the kitty grows up, the children and I refuse to call him Hank. He is LT to us. Terence refuses to call him LT and will only refer to him as Hank. The four of us cannot agree even on his nametag, which, as a result, reads: "LT Hank." So to the vet he becomes Lieutenant Hank.

In the dark days just after Terence's death, it is clear that LT is mourning as well. He prowls the house. I grow sentimental.

"Maybe we should start calling him Hank now?" I suggest to Terry.

Terry's head snaps up.

"No way!" he says. "Dad and I were both very stubborn about that. I'm not going to let him win just because he died."

19

Looking back I ask myself, over and over again: How much of what I did for Terence wasn't really for Terence at all, but for me?

How much of my belief in this clinical trial came from my need to believe? How much did I work to save him because I couldn't imagine life without him? How much was for me? How much was for him?

For during this time of the clinical trials, I needed him more than ever. He was the only thing, I believed, standing between me and madness.

From the moment we had arrived in Philadelphia in the summer of 2003, life promised to be difficult enough even under the best of circumstances. The *Inky* was a feisty, proud paper, well aware of its storied past as an eighteen-time Pulitzer Prize winner and covetous of more. For years before I arrived, the *Inquirer* and its owner, Knight Ridder, had been locked in mortal combat over the proper role of the paper. Was it to cover wars and Washington; to have correspondents in Jerusalem and Johannesburg, in Paris and London, in Tokyo and Beijing? The staff believed its stage was the globe and its audience the world. Knight Ridder—the paper's owner—was alarmed at the hemorrhage of readers at all metro-area papers and was fighting for more coverage at home: libraries, schools, bond issues, Little League, garden clubs. The newsroom was indignant at what it saw as a demeaningly reduced vision of its role. Knight Ridder was scornful of what it saw as the newsroom's self-indulgent self-image.

The result? An odd—but ferocious—civil war. Knight Ridder was constantly furious with its biggest paper, once its biggest moneymaker. The newspaper was in permanent revolt against its owner, rebelling in ways both overt and silent.

When I arrived, the scars of the last decade of this fight were still evident, made worse by recent deep staff cuts. At least, everyone assured me, all that was behind us now. We could make a fresh start, they said. The worst, they said, was over.

The worst, it turns out, was just beginning. Within just a few months, the *Inquirer* took the sad lead in the decline and fall of the American newspaper.

Over the next three years we did manage to eke out some fantastic journalism—the kind that makes me happy to do the work that I do, the kind that Terence was pushing me to do all along. We unearthed illegal activities by a powerful state senator—he eventually went to jail. We so infuriated the Bush/Cheney campaign that they posted my email address on their website, and for weeks I drowned in thousands of hostile emails.

We even brought the world to our doorstep. On Saturday, February 4, 2006, just as Terence and I are about to join the clinical trial, he helped me work through another scary situation. I am the only editor of a major newspaper in the United States to decide to run the Danish cartoon of Mohammed wearing a bomb on his head instead of a turban—the cartoon that causes riots in Europe. By the following Monday, protesters are in front of our building carrying signs with my face and the face of Hitler. Joe Natoli, my publisher, and I plunge into the crowd, shaking hands, talking to families, listening to their stories. The crowd turns friendly. I emerge with several new copies of the Koran. The pride I see on Terence's face—the same pride I saw that long-ago day on the airstrip in Florida—keeps me going, even when I am scared.

Meanwhile at work, I am pulled in impossible directions. It feels, I tell Terence, like being stuck in a bog with a dying, thrashing rhinoceros. Move two-thirds of the staff to the suburbs, comes the order. Cut cellphone bills. Cut out comics. Cut 10 percent of the budget. Cut another 10 percent. Cut another. Make the budget work. Make the paper great again. Reach out to the world. Be the voice of the community. Cut costs. Do great journalism.

All through it there is only one safe spot. One place where I know I am okay. One place where at the end of a day when I feel like I can do nothing right, I feel again as if I can do no wrong. Is it this safe spot that I am protecting? How much do I need Terence to stay alive for me?

Finally the paper—and all of Knight Ridder—dies, and a whole new nightmare begins. By March 2006, just as Terence is beginning his first cycle of Avastin and Nexavar, Knight Ridder is sold, and the *Inquirer* in turn is itself put up for sale.

For the next three months, until June, Terence does another cycle of Avastin and Nexavar. And another. And another. Every month we hold our breath waiting for the scans. Every day at work, slender young investment bankers in black suits with slicked-back hair—these representatives of potential buyers are all men, and all in their thirties, it seems—stride through the newsroom en route to view our PowerPoints in the seventeenth-floor board-room.

The men scribble furiously during the presentations on money. They pull out their BlackBerries and leave the room to refresh their coffee and Diet Coke when I begin my speech about jour-nalism and its importance to the community. I know why I bore them. They want to strip costs from the paper, make it profitable, and resell it. Great journalism? My life's work? Meaningless to them.

Every night I leave exhausted, frantic, and frightened. Every night Terence walks me till I am calm. Just as he did in Beijing.

I worry about the paper. Worry about who will buy it. Worry about how many they will lay off when they do. Worry about the news, the community, the people, the kind of journalism I have spent my life practicing.

What I don't tell Terence is the other thing that worries me.

I worry about my health insurance.

For it is my health insurance, from my succession of newspaper employers, that has paid for Terence's surgery with Dr. Turner. It is my health insurance that paid for his interleukin. For Dr. Pierce. For all those years with Dr. Bukowski. For Providence Portland. The Cleveland Clinic. Presbyterian Hospital.

I am under no illusion about my future with the paper after it is sold. Chances are 99 percent that I will be gone. Rationally, I know I will find a new job. And, rationally, I know about COBRA, the federal law that means that I will be able to buy insurance for eighteen months if my job-related policy suddenly goes away. Terence, at sixty-five, is eligible for Medicare. Rationally, I know all this.

Nonetheless, I am totally, irrationally, completely, and almost paralyzingly fearful. What if something goes wrong? One nano-second of break in our insurance coverage and Terence becomes practically uninsurable. Then the medicine that is keeping him alive is suddenly out of our reach.

What would happen to him then? What would happen to us? What would happen to me?

Is this how all those people across the country are feeling who face diseases like ours without the kind of help we've had all along? For how many people like me and Terence does the loss of a job feel like a death sentence? How many people wind up with no health care to fall back on when something big changes in their lives—as it is about to in ours?

On May 23, 2006—our nineteenth wedding anniversary and the last day of Terence's third cycle on Avastin—the paper is sold. My new boss is a brash, mouthy, blindingly and abrasively self-confident local PR man who has persuaded a group of banks, unions, and local millionaires to put up more than $500 million for what, in a column five days later, I will call "the great experiment."

Cycle after cycle, the drugs appear to be advancing against the cancer. Increasingly, we grow confident. Increasingly, the treatment just becomes part of the background of our lives. Every day Terence takes his Nexavar tablet. Every two weeks he goes for his Avastin drip. Every month we hold our breaths before the CAT scan and exhale in relief when we get the good news.

None of this is without a price. There is nothing of the debilitating wasting, hair loss, and nausea of traditional chemotherapy. Terence is far from debilitated. But the side effects of the drugs, the treatment, and the enervating new routine do get him down.

Terence has small veins. The constant blood draws and needle insertions for the drip are agony.

"They are turning me into a pincushion!" he grouses over dinner one night.

Only one nurse seems to have a gentle touch. She is chubby and cheery. Terence is happy when he sees her and complains loudly to anyone who will listen when she is not available. "Where is my roly-poly friend?" he demands. "I want my roly-poly friend!"

Although nothing like the horror of the IL-2 or traditional chemo, the side effects are nonetheless persistent, vexing, and uncomfortable. There are rashes that embarrass him when they spread to his face. Itching that torments him, especially on his feet. The worst, though, is the constant stomach ailments. Day after day, week after week, month after month Terence struggles with symptoms that are very much like a bad stomach flu.

He is not a good patient.

He breaks the rules of the clinical trials. He shows up when he wants to show up. He cancels when he wants to cancel. Dr. Flaherty and the oncology nurse running the trial, Kathy Harlacker, find out what I have known all along: My headstrong husband expects the world to adapt to him.

Usually it does.

"He showed on numerous occasions how important it was to him to maintain his rules on how to go about life on a day-to-day basis," says Dr. Flaherty. "Kathy would note him as being the most free-willed among our patients in that clinical trial," he says discreetly.

In 2011, I reach Ms. Harlacker at the University of Pennsylvania hospital, where she is still running clinical trials. She is considerably more direct: "I remember your husband well," she writes to me. "He was a very fine gentleman. He pretty much tried to dictate to us how his treatment would go."

Terence loves what the medicine is doing for his cancer, hates what it is doing to his life. Over and over he demands that Dr. Flaherty fix his problems for him. At Terence's command, in an attempt to reduce the side effects, Dr. Flaherty reduces the dose of Avastin in May. In July, he discontinues the Nexavar for two days, hoping that a break will reduce the stomach turmoil. By August they give up on the Nexavar altogether. The side effects abate a bit. The metastases continue to shrink.

It isn't until I have read the records from this period several times that I can confront the question that I have been pushing to the back of my mind: How much did Terence go through this only because he knew I wanted him to?

Did he suffer through this treatment only to protect me and the children? My head knows that wives and husbands and children and parents can cling desperately to their loved ones long after the loved ones themselves are ready to go. Was I so blind that I could not see this in myself? Did my irrational hopes for treatment and more life for him far outweigh his own? I have to wait till my third visit with Dr. Flaherty after Terence has died before I can summon the courage to ask the question.

Dr. Flaherty's answer surprises me.

Terence did want to run the show, Dr. Flaherty says. He did want to make the rules. Naturally, he wanted to stop feeling so bad. But in hours and hours of their conversations together, Dr. Flaherty says he came to realize that Terence also really wanted to be cured. And that Terence really believed he was going to be cured. In fact, says Dr. Flaherty, he believes that Terence may have believed in the cure even more than I did.

The proof, in Dr. Flaherty's mind, is not the violence of Terence's fight against the side effects. To the contrary, Dr. Flaherty says. It is the degree to which he put up with them. Even though they together reduced the doses several times, Dr. Flaherty says, there were many more times when they did not.

"The side effects of the therapy—in his case, that was all investment. That was all him willing to stake that with the idea that he was going to beat the odds. He was pretty free and open about talking about his side effects and was willing to complain about them when needed. But at the end of the day, when I'd say our choices are to maintain where you are or drop the dose and try to make this more tolerable, he'd say, no, let's leave this right where it is. To suffer through side effects that will really limit your ability to do the things you love to do with the hope that that's going to pan out to some better future that might not have been there for you—that's a different way of investing your energy. He was willing to complain, but he wasn't willing to stop or change or take it easy."

I exhale. A weight lifts.

Terence never does stop doing what he loves. Even during his treatment, even on the hardest days, Terence's life is full. He teaches journalism at Drexel. I visit his classes. I watch him teach: Here are the facts, he tells his students. Write four paragraphs. Now write a headline. Now write another four paragraphs. Another headline.

In a navy suit and a red bow tie, he strides back and forth across the front of the room. Write a thirty-second radio script. Write a one-minute radio script. Time's up. Switch papers. Start over. What's on the front page of today's *Philadelphia Inquirer?* Don't know? Then why are you taking this class? Who is Ernie Pyle? Who is I. F. Stone? Don't know? Look them up. Who is Martha Gellhorn? Don't know? You should. Look her up. Write another four paragraphs. Now write eight. Hand them in. What is a gag order? What is prior restraint? Don't know? Go find out.

At home, he studies Arabic.

Why Arabic? I have no idea, except that it is a language he does not know. He is fluent in Chinese and Japanese. I've heard him converse in French and Spanish. He can get by in German and he claims Russian—a claim I cannot substantiate, but one that his cable car buddy Dick Epstein, who later traveled with Terence through Russia in the 1960s, says is true. Arabic—well, that's just enough of a challenge for him. He practices constantly, sitting in front of the History Channel. On the TV screen, the Allies fight back in the Atlantic and the Pacific. Terence sits in our sunny family room, drawing his pen rhythmically across the page. Strange curves and swirls appear. Within weeks his graceful hand is weaving out words, sentences, phrases. His teacher holds up his script to the class in admiration. Day after day I hear him repeating, over and over, the guttural sounds that are so foreign to English speakers.

Then there is his music. He takes up the violin. He practices scales on our grand piano. Every evening I hear him picking through the notes from an adult piano course he keeps on the music stand and sawing his bow through "Walking the Dog" and

"The Country Fiddler" from *Building Technique with Beautiful Music.*

The medicine buys him time with our children. Time with me. It buys him music and study and Sunday afternoons with his friends.

So what else does the medicine buy us, buy him? What else is he doing? What other thoughts and ideas fill his head in what he doesn't yet know will be the last months of his life? Today, there is evidence all around me in the piles of projects he left behind. The stacks of newspapers waiting to be clipped and filed. The bins of 35-millimeter film with his undeveloped pictures— photographic studies of Philadelphia, shots of antique cars, odd bumper stickers. After he dies, I move them all to the basement. I move his instruments—in the bedroom alone there is a double-bell euphonium, a trumpet, two E-flat horns, a sousaphone, a trombone, and a washboard—into a corner. I can now walk around the bed without knocking something over. I vacuum the entire floor for the first time since we moved in five years earlier.

Three years after his death, however, his dresser remains un-touched. I can see the stacks towering at least a foot above the surface. In the sedimentary layers, I can spot photos of his mother, his father, his stepfather. I see a harmonica, a Styrofoam head, union insignia, whole folded newspapers, flash cards, a model Packard, a sousaphone mouthpiece, a model cable car, a recorder, a cornet, a trumpet mute, a Chinese ceramic vase, and a palmetto-style fan with a photo of James Joyce on it.

I must face my fear of dismantling these layers. Once this belonging-sculpture is leveled and I root out the contents of this dresser, the last visual clues to his mind will be gone.

I also must face another of my secret fears. It's a faint one, but real nonetheless. He fiercely guards his private space. I have never opened these drawers. Once I enter them, what will I find?

Will I find evidence after all these years that he really is a spy?
More identities? Perhaps his three names—Laudeman, Rotunno,
Foley—are not the whole story? Will I find a fourth name? A fifth?
Will I find that, like his father, he has concealed another marriage
that I don't know about? Another family? Will I find baby pictures
I don't recognize? Long-preserved letters or legal documents?

I attack the layers slowly. As I work, I write down everything I
find and sort things into piles. Keep. Throw away. Save for the
children. Donate to Goodwill. I must be tough on myself. Nearly
everything I find I want to keep.

Here is the catalog of the things that Terence filled his life with
in his last six months:

San Francisco cable car conductor hat
Agfa box camera
Kazoo
Joke glasses with a nose
Two baby blue angel candle holders
6 rolls of film
Silver baby shoe bank
Calligraphy ink
Gold bow
Valve oil
Leica camera
Two "learn Italian" tapes
Zopkuu camera
Two alarm clocks
Gift-wrapped Chris Thomas King CD of Hurricane Katrina songs
Card from vintage furniture store
3 disposable cameras
Discman
Pocketknife
Arabic flash cards

Admission ticket to Pompeii

Violin bow

Teak box with:

    11 gold pens

    12 pairs of cufflinks

5 boxes of rosin

27 bow ties—some unopened

Unused urine sample cup

Book of checks

Book of check deposit slips

Clippings

    Bush's economics

    Korean war

CD of Bob Dylan's *Highway 61*

CD of Terry's band, The Astronauts

Medication list from August 20, 2007

Boar-bristle clothes brush

Livestrong wristband

Book of souvenir postcards from 1876 Philadelphia

Investigative Reporters and Editors membership card

3 combs

Clothing patch from Oregon City Traditional Jazz Society

Philadelphia musician's union card (Local 77) for 2006/2007

Metal model of a 1950s four-propeller passenger plane

4 watchbands

67 guitar picks

Beer bottle opener

Betty Grable pinup picture

Bagpipe practice pipes

Records and one CD of calliope music

Plastic model kit of the *Titanic*

Boston Globe, April 16, 1912, announcing *Titanic* sinking

Cinderella note cards

Calligraphy set

Plastic folder with 15 parking tickets

CD: *Acting with a British Accent*

CD of Christmas carols

CD of Chinese poetry by Terence Foley

CD set of Jo Stafford

Tape of Howard Zinn on U.S. imperialism and the war with Spain

NY note card (letter inside)

Center City Car Wash member card

Philadelphia Archery and Gun Club membership card from 2005

USAA membership card

Faculty DragonCard (Drexel)

Prescription drug plan card

Frequent photo rewards card from Ritz/Wolf camera stores

Community College of Philadelphia student ID from 2006

Luggage tags

Plane and train receipts

Post-it notes

Postcards (used and unused)

Cough drops

Batteries

Books:

   Easy Japanese

   Japanese-English dictionary

   Pocket-size *King Lear*

   Russian phrasebook

   King James Version of the Bible

   Pocket-size *Macbeth*

   Mao's Little Red Book

   Basic Japanese Conversation

   English-Chinese dictionary

   Getting Along in French

1954 edition of Fenn's Chinese dictionary
The Field Guide to Stains
The Hundred Best Movies
How to Play the Concertina
Instruction books for violin, sax, and trombone
Donald Keene book of Japanese literature
Book on the teaching of Islam
3 harmonicas
5 recorders
1.5-inch harmonica
Flash cards
    French conversation
    Spanish verbs
    Spanish grammar
    French grammar
Red silk flag of communist Vietnam
3 decks of playing cards
Pack of 2 decks of playing cards with dice
Straight razor
Clown head pencil sharpener
Model Norfolk and Western coal car
Model tuba
Pocket watch and chain
BB gun
Arab sheik Halloween costume
Volcanic rock from Mount Vesuvius
Bagpipe chanter
3 juggling balls and a teach yourself juggling book
Gun cleaning set
6 pairs of spectacles
4 money belts
American Dairy Association tie clip

Plants of the Bible playing cards

Booklet: *On Khrushchev's Phony Communism and Its Historical Lessons for the World*

One corner of one drawer has a tiny stash of socks and underwear and handkerchiefs. The three shallow upper drawers have been turned into filing spaces for the index cards that he always carries with him in his left-hand breast pocket. I find them there organized and categorized by subject, each stack rubber-banded and labeled:

Movies to Watch

T2 Movies

Warfare

Boxing

TBF Poetry

Media Stupidity

Entomology

Latin

AP

Christmas Display

TBF Haiku

Story Ideas

Architecture

North Korea

Ph.D.

Jokes

UK Asia Center

China Civ

Interrog.

Medical

Music

Newspaper Clippings

Addresses and Directions
Japanese Flash Cards
Arabic Flash Cards
Notes to Self
Business Cards

To my relief—and disappointment?—there are no stray pay stubs from the CIA. No letters of commendation with Langley return addresses. No testimonials of service recognized by the grateful people of Cuba. Or the Soviet Union. Or China or North Korea for that matter. I find no unexplained photos. No baby pictures except of our own children. No letters from unknown lovers. No rent checks for condos in Florida. No evidence of requests from long-unacknowledged children for belated meetings.

Perhaps there is some evidence somewhere of some mysterious, unspoken, shadowy life that he once lived outside of my view. "No one ever knows one hundred percent of anyone," he is fond of saying. If such an alternate existence existed—and for all his romantic mystery, I doubt there was one—he, like any clever spy, has erased all trace of it. All that is left is the shadow of an outsized personality for whom anything is, if not probable, at least possible.

I will never know.

What I do find, though, is plenty of evidence of the man I *do* know, a man who lives deeply inside his own family. There is Terry's hair from his first cut. A crooked pottery mug made by Georgia. Photos and photos and photos. Our gap-toothed children. Our smiling children. Our sullen children turning from the camera. Our children in overalls. A white Easter hat. Birthday cards from Terry and Georgia from 1999. A sheet of crayoned coupons promising dozens of impossibly virtuous feats for Father's Day.

One thing I find tickles me—something I have already seen a few years earlier. One evening over dinner, he gleefully told

Georgia and Terry and me about finding a doodle that a young woman in his journalism class had accidentally left behind. He showed us the paper, and we all laughed. Now, here, in the bottom of his dresser, three years after his death, I find the doodle again—only now it is carefully trimmed and framed.

It reads: "Terence Foley is hot."

Yet if anything really surprises me, it is the extent of his sentimental attachment to our mutual past. I open a drawer to find a stash of yellowing newspapers. I flip through them to find copies of every news project I have ever directed. Atlanta. Oregon. Lexington. Philly. There is a trade magazine with my picture on the cover. A nude photo of me from 1987 or 1988, discreetly tucked away in a small box. Safely stashed between two layers of cardboard I find our campy wedding photo from China and I remember, just for a second, standing there as the photographer snapped the shot. And there, as well, carefully preserved, I find the business card I handed him on that long-ago day in Beijing, tucked in side by side with one of his own.

As the summer heat spreads through 2006, Terence is getting better and my work is getting harder and harder. Tensions with the new owner are rising. Every night I come home to Terence with the tale of some new, usually unpleasant, twist. I begin to feel the odd, lurching vertigo of riding the waves of big uncontrollable shifts in power. Daily life begins to feel like some HBO special on the Borgias, or perhaps *I, Claudius*. Conversations start and stop depending on who is in the room. Cabals form, dissolve, and re-form again. The neutral middle of satisfying work well done is crushed between the glaring counterpoles of—for some people—ambition unleashed, and for others, despair. Both appear in unexpected places, owned by unexpected people. Each feels equally unsettling. At night, when I can't sleep, Terence walks me up and down the halls of our house. Up and down. Up and down.

And for just that moment, everything is okay.

I am fired on Wednesday, November 8, 2006, one week after Terence begins his ninth cycle of Avastin.

That afternoon, I get a call from Matt Winkler, editor in chief of Bloomberg News.

"So do you know what you are doing next?" he asks me.

"No," I say.

"Well, I do."

Matt is an old friend from my *Wall Street Journal* days. Bloomberg is a once-upstart organization now flexing some big muscles. But how can I work there? It's known for its 6:00 a.m. meetings, sixteen-hour days, and grueling pace. What's more, it's a two-hour commute from home. Each way.

Thrown off one bucking bronco, I'm being asked to jump onto another one and begin another wild ride, this time at a place just as ferociously determined to grow and thrive as the last one was to try not to vanish.

Terence once again steps into the breach.

"Don't worry about a thing at home. I'll handle everything," he says. "Do it."

And so I do.

We live in hope.

20

So what's the cost of all this hope?

That's the big mystery that my colleague Chuck Babcock and I work for six months to discover. Starting in the summer of 2008, and working well past the second anniversary of Terence's death, I fax off requests to hospitals and doctors. Meanwhile, to help us understand what we are looking at, Chuck builds a series of spreadsheets, and I compare what we are seeing with my memories of our experience and my reporting.

You might think that I would have a pretty good idea of the costs of Terence's illness. After all, throughout all of his treatments, the statements from the doctors' offices, from the hospitals, and from the laboratories poured in regularly. Every month also brought a blizzard of envelopes from the insurance companies, the "explanations of benefits" that were supposed to tell me what we had been billed for a service, what the insurance company paid, and what we owed.

At first I think my own messy life is the reason I didn't really have a clue about the costs. I am more than usually disorganized, more than usually perplexed by detail, more than usually panicked when confronted with numbers I don't understand and can't make sense of. And, as Terence got sicker, slowly and subtly I found myself increasingly overwhelmed. I kept the mortgage paid, the lights on, and the kids fed. I kept the car insurance current and the kids' shots up to date. When doctors' bills came with balances on them, I paid them. But tally them up? Figure out who was charging what for what? Untwist the maze of providers and services? Half the time the bills came with names I had never heard of for things I didn't recognize. I had no trouble at first believing I was to blame for my own lack of knowledge.

Yet the more Chuck and I work, the easier it becomes to see why despite the blizzard of paper I received, I had no idea what anything cost. As we leaf through the stack of documents, it is also easy to see why 21 percent of the money spent on health care goes to paperwork and administration. The bills we review are voluminous and often incomprehensible. Some take days to decipher. What does "opdpatins t" or "balxfrded" mean? How can I tell if the dose charged was the same as the dose prescribed?

Chuck and I make nuisances of ourselves with the folks on the other end of the line. Who were these doctors whose names were on the bills? We unearthed bills with complicated corporate names, for health care providers Terence and I never met, for procedures I can't remember happening. Sometimes one visit generated a flurry of bills from a half-dozen different providers. From the doctor. The person who took the scan. The person who read the scan. Sometimes the insurance payments lumped several different things together into one generic heading—like "radiology."

As we work, a strange pattern begins to emerge: We begin to see that some things that should have cost about the same had wildly different price tags. What is going on? Why are our numbers varying so wildly? To try to figure out what was happening, we picked a common, standard procedure: computerized tomography, better known as the CT, or CAT scan. Computerized tomography is a procedure that links a rapid series of X-rays to make a 3-D image of a patient's organs. Terence had been having CAT scans pretty steadily ever since that first day in the emergency room in Oregon when the cancer was discovered. During the Avastin/Nexavar trial, it was the results of the CAT scans that we waited so breathlessly for.

Surely it should be reasonably easy to find out how much we—through my employer's insurance—paid for each one.

Unexpectedly, my messy life turns out to lead us to surprising insights. Because Terence and I moved a lot, Chuck and I can now see what most people never get to see. We can see not only what one hospital charged for the scans, but also what many different hospitals and other providers all across the country charged. And because each move came with a change of employer—and a change of health insurance—we can see something even more interesting: We can see what different insurance companies reimbursed for pretty much the same procedure. By the time he died, Terence had received benefits from four insurers and had undergone procedures in four different states. He was also eligible for Medicare for most of this time, although we never used it.

The first thing that surprises me from our research is simply the sheer number of the procedures that Terence had. If Chuck had asked me how many CAT scans I believed Terence had had, I would have guessed sixteen. One for each cycle of the clinical trial and, say, a half-dozen more throughout the years. Wild guess.

The answer is seventy-six. Seventy-six CAT scans during a seven-year illness. More than ten a year. I'm sure Terence's guess would have been more accurate than mine, but I'm also sure he would have guessed low too. Way low. Some of the scans were ordered by Dr. Pierce, some by Dr. Bukowski, and some by Dr. Flaherty. But many others were ordered in various hospitals across the country, some by doctors we never met for purposes I can't now explain. Since none of us—Terence and me included—had to account for the cost of these procedures, all of us, doctors and patients alike, could casually afford to pop them like cherry Twizzlers.

Were all of them useful and ordered for a good reason? I'm positive of that. Were all of them necessary? I'm just as sure not.

And how much did they cost?

Some scans were done on the old enclosed-tunnel machines. Some on daintier machines that had more open space and made less noise. Some were done "with contrast"—that is, with a special dye used to help see the cancer. Some were done without. Some were done in hospitals, others in stand-alone imaging centers that do nothing else. Overall, though, each of the scans was pretty much the same.

Yet from Portland to Philadelphia, from 2000 to 2007, the price of the procedures ordered by Terence's doctors ranged from $550 in April 2001 at EPIC Imaging in Portland to $3,232 in 2006 and 2007 at the Hospital of the University of Pennsylvania in Philadelphia. In between were charges like $1,252 at St. Joseph Hospital in Lexington, Kentucky, in 2002 and $1,750 at the Cleveland Clinic in 2003.

The most expensive charge was more than twelve times the amount reimbursed by Medicare in 2007, the government health program for the elderly and disabled that is the biggest U.S. payer of medical bills.

What's more, we discovered that the amounts the hospitals and providers billed the insurance companies bore almost no resemblance to the amounts the insurance companies actually paid. And each insurance company made a totally different calculation of what they would pay for the same procedure.

The turmoil at the *Inquirer* provided a startling insight into this fact. Because the *Inquirer*'s new owner immediately changed our health insurance plan, Chuck and I are able to see something strange: what two different insurance companies paid for the same procedure.

In late 2006, following an Avastin cycle, Terence had a scan at the University of Pennsylvania hospital, which billed the insurance company $3,232. My insurer that month was UnitedHealth Group, which paid $2,586.60, or 80 percent of what the hospital asked.

Three months later, another Avastin cycle, another scan. Same patient. Same hospital. Same machine. Same $3,232 bill. The only thing that has changed is that my employer has switched insurance companies. The new insurer, WellPoint Inc.'s Empire Blue Cross and Blue Shield, paid the hospital $775.68, or 24 percent.

At that time, Medicare was reimbursing $250.94 for the same procedure.

And what would someone without insurance pay the University of Pennsylvania hospital for a similar scan? We accidentally found that out too, when a stray record found its way into our pile. This unfortunate person, who was paying the bill out of pocket, paid $1,657—or $881.32 *more* than Blue Cross paid the hospital, and $1,406.06 *more* than Medicare paid.

What did Terence and I pay?

Nothing.

What was this all about? Why did these prices vary so much? And why was what actually got paid so wildly different from hospital to hospital and from insurance company to insurance company?

It takes a lot more calculating, a lot more calling—and something I observed during another trip to China—before I can finally wrap my mind around what was going on.

21

From halfway around the world, I hear the cancer return.

I am standing less than a mile from the place where Terence and I first met when, nearly a quarter of a century later, I hear him coughing.

Thanks to the Avastin, life has been feeling pretty good to all of us as the spring of 2007 turns into summer. Terence continues work on his book of Chinese poetry. He begins writing a screenplay. Terry is playing and singing all over the country with the School of Rock. He and his high school buddies write six songs and burn a CD in one of their living rooms. Georgia becomes a decent tennis player. I rise every day at 4:30 to begin my day at Bloomberg. My new job takes me all over the world. Prague. London. Paris. Madrid. Singapore. And finally, back here to Beijing.

The city where Terence and I met is gone. The years have lifted the darkness from the Boulevard of Heavenly Peace. The eerie blackness that greeted me 8,987 days earlier—the day my first flight here circled the city—is gone. Now neon shouts to the sky, defining streets and boulevards that weren't even imagined in the Peking where Terence and I collided a lifetime ago. Driving in from a flight in the summer of 2007, I see the old linden-lined airport road, shadowy and silent, running under the brand new flyovers and cloverleafs.

Downtown, the horse carts have disappeared. The stone-floored courtyard houses are gone. Even the human wave of bicyclists has nearly vanished, replaced by an even wider and more daunting sea of automobiles. The 1980s' dusty monotony of a city recovering from siege has exploded into a riot of restaurants, karaoke bars, cinemas, and storefronts. Skyscrapers swallow whole neighborhoods.

I host a dinner for our news bureau at the Lan Club, across the street from what was once my home. The restaurant has black crystal Baccarat chandeliers, a cigar bar, five-foot-long sushi boats, walls made from oil paintings, and room after room of artistic kitsch—women's satin shoes abutting rhinoceros heads, Hindu icons and velvet chairs. Over cocktails, I find that one of my new colleagues grew up not far from here. I do some quick mental math and realize that this svelte young woman could easily have been one of the bare-bottomed babies Terence and I saw squatting with their young parents on a summer night on the sidewalk outside my compound. In the China that Terence and I inhabited, uniformed guards with guns stood between us and her. Chic and trim, she orders a Chardonnay.

I can hardly imagine a Chinese nostalgic for those dark days of cold and hunger and monotony. Yet without even realizing it, I am mourning. What for? An era. A vanished moment in history. A lifetime. Do I unconsciously realize what lies ahead? I don't know. I don't think so. I still don't see it coming.

This time around, Terence has no interest in coming with me. He has retreated further and further into the China of the past that he loves so much. He is putting the finishing touches on his book. It is a textbook of classical Chinese poetry, hundreds of poems carefully glossed and explained, with detailed notes on poetic convention through the dynasties. He is the only man I know who knows the Chinese words for "amino acids" and "artificial insemination" as well as "alliteration" and "onomatopoeia." A Kinko's box marked "ChinaPo—Good Copy" still sits on my desk. He had been lending his book out to Chinese professors around the country to use in their classes, and this is a copy that remained.

My trip takes place at the end of August, summer vacation, which is why Georgia is here too. She hasn't been back to China since the day she left as a Mandarin-speaking almost-four-year-old. Now at thirteen she is an extraordinarily self-sufficient young woman. I have long, grueling days of work during which she is alone. A week later in Tokyo, I will leave her in our hotel room with money, movies, and permission to call room service. When I return at the end of the day I find the beds covered instead with an array of takeout sushi, pastries, bottled soda, chips, and nail polish in unfamiliar colors.

"How did you do that?" I ask.

She barely looks up.

"Pointing," she says.

In Beijing while I am at work, she visits with friends of my friends from the past. She tours the Forbidden City and the Great Wall. She shops. Terence and I have filled her with stories of the poverty, the oppression, the lack of opportunity that causes young Chinese women to give up their daughters. On this trip, our speeches' messages are crushed in a hail of Gucci, Chanel, and Coach knockoffs.

The country of her birth has vanished.

I take her by the Jianguo Hotel to see Daddy's old room. The Chinese words for the room number: SI-ER-*san*—423—the first two syllables emphatic, the third lilting—are burned into my memory. The hotel, once a palace of luxury amid the Beijing gloom, now feels seedy and downcast, like one of those lost and abandoned motels on the drive to Florida along Route 1. Time has passed both by. Georgia is bored. We photograph the door to show Daddy. Every night we call him to tell him the news.

On Monday, September 3, 2007, on one of these calls, I hear the cough.

"You should get that checked out," I say.

I am not worried. I am not even vaguely concerned. I am thinking Claritin or NyQuil. It never occurs to me that here in Beijing, barely half a mile away from where we began, I am hearing the beginning of the end. It is twenty-four years to the day from that long-ago party where I met that would-be Soviet expert.

Four days after our phone call, on Friday evening, September 7, 2007, Terence and Terry, bouquets of daisies in hand, meet Georgia and me at Philadelphia International Airport as we step off our seventeen-hour flight home. We stop for dinner at our favorite Indian restaurant and ask a passerby to snap a photo. The stranger catches Terence and me grinning. Terry's auburn hair flames copper in the last of the day's sun. Georgia is lithe and lovely, almost an adult. Terence is round faced, robust, and cheery, his pocket stuffed with his usual index cards. We all look relaxed and happy. "Yep," says Terry when he sees the photo later. "Everyone is right with the program."

Terence coughs through dinner.

The following weekend, Terence and I fly together to Detroit for a retirement party.

By then he knows that his cough is caused by an unexpected growth in one of the cancerous spots. He learns the result of an earlier scan: One of the spots that the Avastin has hollowed out is filling back up with cancerous cells. The new growth is irritating his throat. Dr. Flaherty calls it a "refill," Terence says. I feel bad for him that the cough is so annoying. Beyond that, I feel no real concern at all. More than six years have passed since we first saw the shadow. We have been through this before. We have dodged death three times before.

Why not a fourth?

Our party is a warm, intimate gathering of old friends. Janet, a professor of folklore. Her husband, Andrea, an Italian professor and lover of Dante Alighieri. Their daughter Mia, a chef. Our friend Katy, a papyrologist. Katy's husband, Linos, whose retirement from General Motors we are celebrating. These are our people. The house is snug and cozy. There is plenty of wine. Andrea fills the house with the smell of Italian cooking. We dip our bread in olive oil and laugh at nothing.

Only one thought darkens my pleasure at this gathering of old friends. That is my fear that it will be our last. My fear is not for Terence. It is for Janet. After many years, Janet's own breast cancer has returned. She and Terence murmur in the other room as Andrea and I chat. I memorize the details of the room. I mull over my pleasure in our shared past. I listen to Andrea and watch Mia, studying for clues that will help me later. What will my life be like when she is gone? How will I be a friend to her and her family? How will I console Andrea and Mia when Janet is gone?

Terence coughs through dinner.

Do I miss something? Do Janet and Terence, in that quiet moment off in her book-filled living room, each confess to the other their fears for the future? Does Terence know more about what is ahead than I do?

Janet says no. She and Andrea both remember an evening of everyday conversation—talking with Terence about some nearby relatives, about their fathers, and music and books. Off in the living room, she and Terence compare notes. They talk about their treatments. There are no cosmic moments. Janet remembers feeling that Terence sees this recurrence, as I do, as just one more issue to deal with. "I do remember that we agreed that the whole thing was a bitch, but that we were going to have one hell of a party and enjoy ourselves," says Janet.

The fall is busy for the whole family. Georgia starts eighth grade. Terry begins college. Terence plunges back into a regimen that we believe will help him beat back the cancer once more. We hope that the annoying spot can be lasered out to give him some relief. Meantime, our best plan is to resume Avastin treatment.

I mentally pause at this point.

Resume Avastin.

Resume?

When Terence tells me that this is the plan, I have to stop myself from crying out. Resume? For much as I torment my mind, I cannot recall his decision to stop. Yes, he says, matter-of-factly. He stopped back in May. I know now from my conversations with Dr. Flaherty that Terence believed he would be cured. Did he believe that he already was cured? Did he believe in the cure, not too little, but too much?

After a year without any growth in the tumors, Dr. Flaherty and Terence decided that it was safe to give him a break from the fatigue, stomach distress, and itching that so bothered him. Did Terence tell me? Did I not pay attention? Did I know at one point and simply forget? Or is it possible that this is just one decision he needed to make alone?

I'll never know.

By the time he tells me, the metastases are back and Terence is blaming his choice. Not to worry, Dr. Flaherty says. Avastin has worked once. Avastin will work again. On September 17, 2007, Terence resumes his Avastin drip. For six weeks in a row he returns to the hospital. An Avastin drip on October 1. One on October 15 and one on October 29.

This time Terence is no longer a part of a clinical trial. When he leaves the test in May, he can't go back on it. That means the drugs are no longer provided free by the maker. A lot of paper-work, explanations, and reports from Dr. Flaherty and Terence get the drug on an "off-label" basis. That means that Dr. Flaherty can prescribe it for a patient he believes will benefit from it, even though it still isn't approved by the FDA for kidney cancer. That also means our insurance company will pay for it.

Which is a very good thing, it turns out.

A look at our insurance records from that time shows why these new drugs are so controversial.

Starting in the month of October, the first month when Ter-ence takes Avastin as a patient and not as a trial subject, Blue Cross is billed $109,440—or $27,360 for each of the four doses of Avastin Terence receives. Each dose costs more than the entire surgery to remove his kidney did back in 2001. As it does with all the other bills, the insurance company negotiates down the actual payment to $6,665.40 a dose, or $26,661 for the four doses. Again, we pay nothing.

I don't get it. If the insurance company can negotiate a price cut of more than $20,000 a dose, then where does the rest of the money go? And why do hospitals and doctors and other health care providers sometimes take 20 percent of what they ask and sometimes 80 percent?

My head spins.

Since Avastin is the single biggest cost of Terence's entire treat-ment, Chuck and I try to find out what the "real" price is.

First off, we try Genentech, which makes the drug. Back in 2006 and 2007, Genentech was charging wholesale distributors $550 for 100 milligrams of Avastin. Based on Genentech's pricing, Terence's 350 milligram dose of Avastin should have been $1,925, or less than one-fourth the amount the hospital charged, and a third of what they actually got from the insurance company. And Genentech says it can't help what anyone decides to charge for the medicine it makes.

What gives?

The hospital says it can't say. It says its contracts with the insurance companies prevent it from discussing the discounts it negotiates. The insurance companies say the same thing. What's more, the hospital says it wouldn't be good to tell patients what the charges are anyway, the way some places do. There would be "hundreds of thousands" of items, says a spokeswoman for the hospital, and seeing those numbers "would not benefit our patients." Instead, she says in an email, the hospital has "specialized staff" to speak with patients about costs of the care.

I still don't get it.

I understand the concept of discounting. I understand the concept of bargaining. I've bought several cars and sat tapping my fingers while the unctuous salesman goes off somewhere to see if the mysterious, unseen "boss" will approve this "deal."

But $20,000 a dose?

Negotiated down to three doses for the price of one?

Suddenly my mind flashes back to China. To Georgia in China. To Georgia in China bargaining in the Silk Market downtown. The vendors waving fake Chanel purses shout out ludicrous prices: "Two thousand yuan!" they cry—$300! What a bargain! Cheap! Cheap!

Why would they ask such a silly price for such an obvious imitation? What a dumb thing to do, I think to myself. Yet I realize the logic of their tactics a few minutes later when I overhear a happy tourist group leaving the market.

"I got it for two hundred yuan!" one woman is exclaiming. She is clutching the same purse Georgia has just bargained down from two thousand to twenty.

I think health insurance works just like that behind the scenes. The payers and the providers are bargaining like car salesmen or Chinese vendors—naming ridiculous prices that have no bearing on reality, hoping that some won't drive such hard bargains.

And the only ones who can't see what is going on are the people like Terence and me who are using the care, and the employers like mine who are paying the bills.

Terence never knew any of this, of course. He knew neither what was billed nor what was paid. I wonder now what he would have thought if he realized that the life-extending one-hour drip was billed at the cost of half an Ivy League tuition every time he sat down. I try to imagine his reaction. He had a way of expressing surprise that annoyed me when he pulled it on me because it could be so theatrical. His jaw dropped like a marionette's. His eyes widened in comic astonishment. I can see him sitting there with the IV in his arm, laying aside his Chinese or Latin or French or Spanish vocabulary cards, and contorting his face in horror. The drugs have saved his life. They may do so again. Yet in my mind he is furious at the cost.

"Morons! Thieves!" I can hear the rant.

Yet would he have done anything different?

22

Over the next few weeks, we gear up for the next phase of our fight. I am impatient and irritable, not anxious.

Impatient? As we wend our way through the new Avastin cycles, we both tap our fingers, look at our watches, review the calendar, and anxiously wait for the drug's effects to kick in. Because the cough, the side effects, and the fatigue are making him miserable, Terence can't wait to feel better. I am looking ahead to dates in our lives and planning when we will get back to normal. By Christmas, certainly, I think. And Thanksgiving? Even that might be reasonable. By the time the family descends on us, things should be stabilized. Do I dare plan on a more ambitious timetable? We have a theater date with the Pulitzer Prize board in the middle of November. Surely he will be well enough to do that. I RSVP back a yes for both of us. I have been asked to give a speech in Dubai at about the same time. It would be great if he could come with me. That's probably pushing things. I plan to go alone.

Irritable? Whenever I am with the doctors, I am always impressed with what they know. How they try to include us in the discussions. How sincere they appear.

But their world? The world they—or someone—has constructed around them? It is impossible. A labyrinth. A fortress. A Rubik's Cube. I exhaust all metaphors in frustration. Each doctor's practice is set up for him or her. They have their own days of the week. Their own receptionists. Their own appointment protocols and their own billing systems. Some of them have their own companies with their own weird names. They're all working in ways that are best for them. It hardly ever seems that they are working together in ways that are good for us.

Over the years, this kind of thing is yet another subject Terence and I clash over.

"Goddammit!" I hear him shouting over the phone, pounding his fist on the counter. "I don't WANT to press one. I want you to help me. Now!"

"These systems have been designed for THEM, not for us," he rails—at me, now, not the phone. "They are designed to keep us away from them, so they can do their own little work without us bothering them. I'm the CUSTOMER, goddammit. I'm why they are in business."

I chide him for his impatience—and selfishness. I see the other side. As editor of a large newspaper, I know all too well that one angry caller may in fact be just one of two, or ten, or fifty—or even a thousand callers, each with the same issue. Each believing himself or herself unique.

"I don't think it's unreasonable to—"

Terence cuts me off.

"Who designed this system? I want the name. Which person? I want to know whose fault this is."

He wants someone to call. Someone to talk to. Someone to throttle.

"Terence!" I am exasperated. "There isn't any one person; it's a system."

That enrages him all the more.

"That's what Kafka writes about," he yells. "Everyone's evading, ducking and weaving. There's no one to blame. No one takes responsibility. Everyone is JUST DOING HIS JOB."

His voice drips with sarcasm, his tone coils upward.

Now I see what he means. I never do find anyone to blame. Each individual person I find is completely reasonable and caring—

often going far beyond what he or she needs to do. But today, looking back over those weeks, there is no question in my mind: This system isn't designed for me and Terence. It is designed for them. I spend days, hours, punching in "1," sitting on hold. Waiting for a callback. Scrolling websites, reading biographies—trying to figure out who the doctors are we are dealing with, whom we should be dealing with, and how we get through to them.

As October draws to an end, the leaves on the redbud in our back courtyard yellow and drop. The school year unfolds with its rhythms of permission slips, homework checks, and music practices. The side effects of Terence's treatments begin to mark the edges of our world. Yet despite his discomfort, our life is still more or less normal. I still get up every morning and go to work at Bloomberg. He still takes the kids to school and picks me up from the train. He is still playing the violin and the piano and practicing his Arabic. He has even started a new project, a screenplay about a murder in Beijing.

Yet his cough is not abating. We try Robitussin. We try Mucinex. I brew him my old favorite: lemon, honey, and bourbon. He coughs, and coughs, and coughs. Dr. Flaherty prescribes something stronger, a cough syrup with codeine. Terence coughs and coughs. We try a purple inhaler. Another prescription for something we call "pearls"—Tessalon Perle, I later learn is the real name. Benzonatate. It's used for people with emphysema, asthma. Serious stuff. It is supposed to hinder the lung reflex that makes you want to cough. It doesn't. He coughs and coughs and coughs and coughs. I look at the latest prescription, something Terence says everyone promises will definitely help. It's OxyContin, an opiate.

Woody Boyd comes to visit. Terence sits in the car with him. He blows his cornet and coughs and coughs and coughs.

Food tastes funny to Terence. Another side effect, I guess. His weight is dropping. He's hardly skeletal, but his clothes are starting to look baggy. Yet we're still keeping close to a normal routine. He even still shops for groceries. He uses one of those little red electric three-wheel carts with baskets that they keep for old folks to use at Superfresh. The kids and I tease him. He tries to run us down.

He's exhausted all the time. It's no wonder, I think. The constant cough alone is surely enough to tire him out. The pain must be wearing. OxyContin is the twentieth-century opium. No wonder he is tired.

I troll the Internet looking for salves and ointments for the skin rashes and lesions that are beginning to cause him so much pain. His biggest complaint, though, is his gut. The medicine, or something, is making him so sick that he is now miserable all the time. Clearly his intestinal surgery from seven years ago is making the side effects worse. I want someone to figure out if there is something else we can do to help him.

And so I find myself in a giant game of hot potato. For the first time since Terence's illness begins I am short-tempered and demanding. He's being treated for cancer. That's Dr. Flaherty's job. How about the tumor that is making him cough? That will be seen by another specialist, Dr. Ali Musani. When can Dr. Musani see us? We don't know. Dr. Flaherty is working behind the scenes. Is Terence's earlier intestinal problem making the side effects worse? I want to know. I call the doctor who treated him earlier for that condition. He is a surgeon. The after-effects are not his business, I learn. Besides, his next available free spot is in two months, his receptionist informs me. I try to explain my concern. Can't we even talk?

Long silence.

December 7?

He's sick NOW, goddammit. I want to see someone NOW.

What about the skin lesions that are tormenting him? We need to see a palliative care specialist. Or a dermatologist. Each time, I begin the conversation anew with someone on the phone. Each time I hear the long pause as someone consults the appointment book for new patients. February? one suggests. Explain the problem to me and I'll have the nurse call you back. Who is referring you to this office? Are you a patient of the doctor's?

I know that throughout Terence's illness his doctors have been communicating with one another behind the scenes. Surely this maze makes more sense to them than it does to me. When I look at the records, I see the professionally dictated, precise notes they sent one another. But right now I want the system to make sense to ME. I want someone to talk to ME. Terence is hurting and I want it to stop. Yet his entire digestive system—from his mouth to his tail—seems to be cut up into separate duchies, each ruled by a separate monarch. The skin? His throat? His lungs? His cancer? All different lands, different kingdoms. And I lack the keys to these kingdoms. They are remote, inaccessible, cut off from me by schedulers and voice mail. I cannot link them together. I cannot even reach them.

Perhaps my quest is misguided. Perhaps none of these people can help after all. Perhaps we are already doing the best we can. Perhaps I should relax and let the professionals do their work. But it feels as if I am the only person seeing Terence. Terence Bryan Foley. A whole person who is hurting, not just a single piece of his body that needs attention. I am frustrated and angry. I want someone to talk to me. NOW.

In the last week of October, Terence calls me at work.

"I can't pick up Georgia at school," he says. "I can't get out of the chair."

I rush home. I am two hours away. I am on my phone the entire trip, cursing the tunnels that cut me off. A friend's mother picks up Georgia. I talk to Terence all the way home.

It is clear I cannot be that far away anymore. I begin working from the guest room. Professionally, the world around us is fracturing. A financial crisis is unfolding. Cellphone in hand, I massage his back and rub cream into his painful skin sores. In my ear I hear chatter about LIBOR and special purpose vehicles and bad banks and good banks, and Hank Paulson and Ben Bernanke and Alt-A mortgages and bad collateral and write-offs. While Terence sleeps I edit stories.

Why do I go into this overdrive? Why don't I just stop? I keep going—with work, with the kids' school, with caring for him—because I don't see this as the end. I see this as our new life. I may be crazy enough to think he will get better; I am not crazy enough to think it will be quick. I am establishing the new rhythms of what I believe will be a way we will have to live for a long time to come.

On Halloween night for the first time ever we leave the candy on the doorstep. His Dracula costume stays wrapped in the basement. Finally we get an appointment with Dr. Musani. Now things will improve, I think. Dr. Musani will laser out the spot. The coughing will stop. Terence will begin to get some sleep. He will stop taking the powerful medications. He will begin to get stronger. The Avastin will work its magic. And life as we knew it will resume.

On Thursday, November 8, 2007, I drive Terence across town to the University of Pennsylvania hospital for our 10:00 a.m. appointment with Dr. Musani. Terence is feeling very weak. The long bridge across the roadway from the parking garage to the offices is impossible for him to negotiate. For the first time, I see the wheelchairs by the elevators in the garage and realize what they are for. I push him into a waiting room. A nurse does the usual blood pressure and pulse thing and sits him on an examining table.

Terence is exhausted. So worn out he cannot sit upright. He twists and squirms on the table, tries to make himself comfortable, tries to lie down. I pull the table extension out. He can't get comfortable. I help him down from the table. He lies down right there on the examining room floor. I bundle his jacket under his head and cover him with my coat.

Dr. Musani enters the room. He is a specialist, an interventional pulmonologist. I am not sure what that means, but Dr. Flaherty tells us that if anyone can remove the lump in Terence's throat it's Dr. Musani. We have never met Dr. Musani before. He seems shy. Seeing his patient lying on the floor, he is also clearly alarmed. This is obviously not what he expected. If Terence is so ill he can't sit up, he belongs in the hospital, not at home. As Dr. Musani leaves to begin the paperwork, he turns to me.

"Have you considered hospice?" he says.

I brush him off. Hospice is for those who are expected to live less than six months. That's not Terence. That's not us.

"We're waiting for the Avastin to kick in," I explain.

Later, Dr. Musani will tell Dr. Flaherty that there is nothing he can do.

We wait in Dr. Musani's examining room for what seems like forever. Finally an aide arrives with a wheelchair, and at 2:24 p.m. Terence is admitted to Rhoads 3, the advanced medical oncology unit.

23

Terence spends the next four days in the University of Pennsylvania hospital.

A battle rages around him, and me.

It is a silent battle. A battle where the opposing sides never face
each other and take aim. It is a battle fought largely through me.
It is a battle I see clearly only in retrospect.

On one side are Dr. Flaherty and me. On the other, the doctors
and nurses and—for all I know—the orderlies, assistants, and the
nice ladies who bring him lunch. The field of battle: Terence.

Is Terence dying or not?

Subtly, I feel the doctors' motivations part. Are we plumping
Terence back up to resume the fight? Or simply easing the decline of a dying man heading to the end? I can feel the question
hover in the air around me.

Dr. Flaherty and I both believe that there is life ahead. Both of
us believe—and I think Terence does too—that we can tame
Terence's illness, that victory is possible. In retrospect, and in
closely reading the medical records, I can see that everyone on
the hospital staff thinks we are crazy. They see a man with his foot
firmly planted on the road to the end.

But to me, their actions speak louder than the words they never
say. If Terence is dying, then why is this medical machine kicking
into such high gear? I know why Dr. Flaherty and I are doing what
we do. We believe we are going to save him. But if the folks in the

hospital believe he is dying—and quickly—then why are they spending so much time, energy, and money to save him?

Today, three and a half years later, I review the medical records—169 pages of them from those four days. Just over 40 pages a day. My memory conjures up these four days as a whirlwind of people, faces, and procedures. People come and go. They politely introduce themselves, explain who they are. I've never seen any of them before. I just as promptly forget their names and become confused.

Who are you again? What do you do? What is your role here? I struggle with the names. I struggle with their functions. I struggle to figure out who's in charge. Susan Domchek? She's the attending. Does that mean she's the boss? I keep asking to meet her. I'm sure I do meet her at some point, but I have no clear recollection. She signs a lot of the documents. She's important in the paperwork but not in our real lives, it appears. So if she's not the boss, who is? Elliot Jerud. He's signing a lot of things too. Does that mean he's the boss? Are you both the boss? Which one of you is in charge here? And how do I know? Who is ordering all these tests? These scans? Are you guys all talking to Dr. Flaherty? To Dr. Musani? To one another? To me?

The doctors all pop in and out of the room at unexpected times. I am sure their visit schedule works with their own lives and work. Not with mine, though. I go home at night to sleep; there is no one else to care for Georgia and get her to school. I drop her off and come straight to the hospital. By the time I arrive a little after eight, someone important has already been by with some medical message that a drowsy and irritable Terence tries to pass on to me.

And a lot of things are going on. He has his blood drawn, eight times. Urine collected, at least twice that I can see. There is a CAT scan of his chest and an MRI of his brain. A physical therapist drops by several times. A nutritionist talks about cancer fatigue, decompensation, and calorie needs. She orders little containers of high-protein drinks to be delivered with his trays; on the way in and out of the hospital, I stop at Potbelly for takeout vanilla shakes to mix with the prescribed protein. Terence refuses to drink them. The protein drinks, he says, only spoil the flavor of the shakes.

And there are drugs. Lots and lots and lots of drugs. Most of them I know about. Some of them I will learn about only by reading the records years later.

Three years after Terence's death, an acquaintance, a hospice chaplain, tells me of hospice workers' black humor about this phenomenon, about how the medical machine keeps on ordering tests and procedures on dying patients. She tells a dark little joke: An orderly goes to the hospital morgue to retrieve a body. It's not there. Instead, he finds a note: Gone to X-ray, it reads.

By day two, after some intravenous fluid and a glucose drip, Terence is feeling a little better. A brisk, cheerful nurse enters the room.

"Good morning, Terence!" she chirps.

"Do I know you?" he growls. "Have we been introduced?"

She is puzzled.

"I don't remember giving you permission to call me by my first name," he says. "The name is MISTER Foley."

Later in the day a doctor stops by. Is it a resident? An intern practicing taking histories? An actual M.D.? I have no idea. The visits all start out the same.

"I'd like to ask you a few questions..."

Terence is snappish. He's been here before.

"I am STILL Terence B. Foley," he says. "I am STILL sixty-seven years old. I STILL was diagnosed with kidney cancer in 2001. Don't you guys ever talk to each other?"

I understand his frustration.

Over and over again since his diagnosis, we have told the same

story to different people. Sometimes they are paying close attention. Sometimes they are going through the motions. Who is
reading these records? Does the next person read what the last
one wrote? Sometimes it appears they do, and sometimes not.

Reading over the records I discover one thing I didn't know:
Terence is diabetic. Over and over again his blood sugar reading
is high. Not surprising. He has been overweight for as long as I've
known him. Perhaps, given his more serious problems, the doctors felt that wasn't important to tell us, or perhaps it was just a
side effect of his many treatments. But I can't help wondering:
Did no one tell us because amid all the specialists we had, no one
was in charge of his blood sugar?

Some records have tiny errors in them. Nothing serious. Just
the small careless differences that come from passing information
among so many people, or from asking Terence or me questions
when we were bored or distracted, or just not really paying attention. One morning's version of the records says his mother died of
breast cancer. Later that day, another account is accurate—she
died of non-Hodgkin's lymphoma. One record says she died in
1971. Another, correctly, says 1986.

At least one record is absolutely accurate. Someone takes some
kind of social adaptation history. The question: What helps you
relieve stress? His answer: Reading. What are the symptoms dis-
played when stressed? Says Terence: I yell at someone. The answer is carefully recorded in his records.

So how many different people look in on Terence during these
four days in the hospital? Reviewing the records today, I find the
names of twenty-seven people, including nine with M.D. after
their signatures:

Susan Domchek, M.D.
Elliot Jerud, M.D.

Hanhngo, R.N.

Neil Wimmer, M.D.

Francis Wilson, M.D.

Anila George, R.N.

Helena Yu, M.D.

Tiffany Gehringer, R.N.

Jeffrey Arkles, M.D.

Maureen Hufford, R.N.

Larissa Shelton, R.N.

Heidi Kapustka, R.N.

John Woo, M.D.

Andrew Bowen, M.D.

Nondas Davis, C.N.A.

Warren Gefter, M.D.

Robert Tabak, pastoral care

Audrey Caspar-Clark, L.D.N., R.D.

Ashley Adams, transition manager (social work intern)

Deborah Lowenstein, L.S.W.

Cathleen Ross-Fredericks, discharge manager

Steve Chickman, Praxair

Jonathan McCaffrey, P.T.

Joan Coynern referred for Penn Care at home

Melissa Maynard, R.N.

Wanda Warren, U.C.

Kathy Zegan, R.N.

That clearly isn't everyone we see, as the lab technicians aren't included, nor the orderlies who push Terence down for more scans, nor the nice ladies who deliver the meal trays and empty the trash and deliver fresh towels.

It isn't hard to see why health care takes up 17 percent of our country's economy. It isn't hard to see how all these costs add up.

. . .

On November 11, before discharging him, a doctor props one of Terence's scans on a light board so I can clearly see the blizzard of white spots, hundreds of tumors covering his lungs.

"There's been substantial progression," he tells me.

Substantial? I'm alarmed. I've just been talking to Dr. Flaherty, and he tells me there has been "some" progression. Which is it?

Without ever breaking professional courtesy or discretion, each manages to convey just how wrong he believes the other to be.

"These specialists see things theoretically," says the hospital doctor. "Sometimes they can't see the patient in context, what he looks like when he's in the hospital."

Says Dr. Flaherty: The folks in the hospital—interns, residents, and fellows—don't see that many cancer patients OUTSIDE of the hospital. And they don't see that many with metastatic kidney cancer—maybe 0.1 percent of their cases. They don't understand that the course of kidney cancer in the lungs is different from that of actual lung cancer.

So Dr. Flaherty is not fazed by the growth. In any case, he and I want to move on to the next link in the daisy chain of newly available drugs. Sutent, another targeted therapy, has been approved for a year. It works as Avastin does, by stopping cancer's ability to build extra blood vessels to feed its growth, but in a different way. One two-hundred-dollar pill a day. A shot at more life. Sutent might have more serious side effects—rashes, fatigue, stomach distress, strokes—but Terence is game. He begins taking it on November 15.

Dr. Flaherty is optimistic about Terence's chances. He's seen Sutent do remarkable things with even sicker patients. He expects it will do the same for Terence.

"Tell Terence that happier days are just ahead," says Dr. Flaherty.

24

Terence believes Dr. Flaherty, I am sure.

In retrospect, I realize that he is starting to believe something else as well. Just home from the hospital, he draws a line down the middle of a sheet of paper. On one side, he orders me to list things to throw away. On the other, things to keep. I won't hear it.

"Stop it!" I snap. "You're not going to die."

"Just do it," he says.

We begin holding two contradictory thoughts in our minds at once. The latest copy of our will has been languishing in a pile of paperwork for more than a year. On November 15, we head downtown to sign it. I drop him at the door then head to park the car. When I return he is so tired, he can barely make it up to the lawyer's lobby. Still proud, he won't use the walker outside of the house. He leans on his cane.

The attorney in charge is my friend Abbe. Three years later, over dinner, I ask her: When you saw him that day, did you know what I wouldn't admit? Did you see that he was going to die?

She doesn't hesitate for a second.

"Absolutely!" she says.

And then she stops. She is remembering something.

Abbe is a taut, professional, politically connected Philadelphia lawyer. Yet I remember seeing her dissolve in tears several years earlier at a social gathering of women as she talked about her mother's then-recent death. Now she is remembering her mother.

"We knew my mother was dying," she says, slowly. "Yet somehow I talked myself into thinking it would be okay to go on the vacation we had planned." No sooner did her family arrive in Hawaii than she got the call. She barely made it back in time, and only one of her two children made the flight.

"How did I think it was okay to leave?" she now asks herself. "What was I thinking?"

As we talk, we realize together that she was thinking what I was thinking: I see this. I understand this. I can't believe this.

She knew her mother was dying. She simply couldn't believe it. "I was just unable to imagine the earth without her in it."

I know the feeling.

Thanksgiving comes. Cousins Margo and Glenn arrive with Miles and Jane, their children, who are just a few years older than Terry and Georgia. Later, after Terence's death, I ask Margo: Did you make the eleven-hour drive from Cincinnati to Philadelphia because you suspected he was dying? No, she says. We knew he was very sick. We didn't know he was dying.

We turn the Thanksgiving kitchen into a war zone of pies. Pumpkin pies. Apple pies. Cherry pies. Margo, Jane, Georgia, and I roll and knead and chop and slice. Lemon meringue. Key lime. Pecan. Hardly traditional Thanksgiving fare. No matter. Whatever anyone wants, we bake. In the living room, Glenn sits at the grand piano. "Ain't Misbehavin'." "On the Sunny Side of the Street." "Take the A Train." Terry lugs a snare drum up from the basement. The only clue that something is different this year is that it is Cousin Miles, not Terence, on the bass fiddle. Terence sits and watches.

Later that evening, we play charades as usual. Terence plays only one round, from his chair, then settles back to watch.

Margo takes one last picture of Terence, sitting on our sofa in the family room. It is easy to see how we can all fool ourselves into feeling...if not normal, then almost. Terence looks tired, sitting there in his familiar red plaid shirt. His glasses are off. His face is a bit flushed, and a tad thinner than usual. But mostly he just looks like Terence.

As Margo, Jane, Georgia, and I clean up, and Terry and Miles mess around with their music in the living room, Terence talks intently with Glenn. After I help him up the stairs to bed, he recounts the conversation.

"Glenn and I agreed on one thing. We have had terrific lives. Whenever we go it will be okay," he says. Yet he adds: "And whenever we go we'll feel ripped off that we didn't get more."

That feels right to me.

He continues. "We also agreed that we are incredibly lucky in our wives. Neither of us can believe how lucky we are. Margo is such a dear," Terence says. And, he adds, Glenn returned the compliment: "'Who wouldn't want to be married to Amanda?'" Terence reports that Glenn says.

Terence tells me this with pride.

It is only much later that I realize what a gift Glenn has given Terence, and Terence, in turn, has given me.

Sitting on that same sofa a few days later, after Margo and Glenn have gone home, I suddenly panic. We've been tempting fate. All along we've been focusing on Terence. What if he winds up fine and I do not? What if I suddenly die and he lives on? Who will care for him and the children? I realize we haven't planned for that chance at all.

"If I'm hit by a truck, I want you to marry Alix," I say. "She will take care of you and the kids."

My sister has a huge heart. She is divorced. She has two daughters Georgia and Terry's age. She is smart and witty.

"You want me to MARRY Auntie Alix?" he asks. He does his annoying dropped-jaw you're-a-moron astonishment face.

I stop to consider. I think about the things Terence and I fight about, still. The piles of projects. The cabinets stuffed till they cannot close. I think about our basement. Boxes of twenty-five-year-old videos splitting open and spilling over the basement floor. Darkroom equipment. Punching bags. The stacks and masses of mingled things that I am only able to inventory slowly in the years after his death: Six jars of mustard. Fourteen Phillips head screwdrivers. A band saw, twenty-one extension cords. Cases of emergency food dating back to 1993. Books on building bird-houses. Boxes labeled "Medieval music." "Passion plays."

I pause and think. Auntie Alix, my generous, funny, red-headed sister, is an obsessive tidier. Closets organized with related items in little baskets. Towels stacked by color, all folds facing the same direction. Her two-car garage actually has room for two cars. Tools aren't in mountains; each is precisely hung. There is no clutter in her house. I stop giving her gifts. It's more efficient to send them straight to Goodwill, I tell her, after spotting a present in the giveaway pile barely a month later. The family jokes that it isn't safe to put our purses down when we visit her house, lest she toss them out while we are eating.

"Okay," I say. "Bad idea."

In the meantime, Terence's face has gone white.

"Don't ever talk about that again," he says.

"About what?"

"You are the center of my life," he says. "If anything happened to you, the light would go out in my world. Don't ever talk to me about it again."

So he knew, I think later, what it would be like once he was gone and I was alone. He knew what it would feel like. We never speak about the end—of either of us—again.

· · ·

I continue my preparations for what I expect will be this new, tougher phase of our life. I find the protein drinks online. I order a case. There is a bodybuilding shop near my office. I buy protein bars in all flavors, dozens of them. From the Philadelphia Parking Authority, I get forms for a handicapped license plate and download the application to get a parking spot right in front of our house.

Each day it is harder and harder to get him up and down the stairs. He has lost weight, but he is still a big man. I begin to research installing a stair lift. Yes, there will be room for one, even in the curving staircase of our Philadelphia rowhouse. Meantime, he lives upstairs. I bring food up to him.

He is no longer able to get in and out of bed alone so I hire a health aide. The woman the agency sends is as close to perfect as I could ask—a quiet, cheerful, religious older island woman with a soft and delicate accent.

I try to make Terence eat. He hates the taste of the protein shakes. I add vanilla. I add ice cream. He hates the protein bars too. I slice them into tiny pieces and try to get him to eat a sliver at a time. Whatever he craves, I buy. Cold grapefruit slices. Chicken noodle soup. Clam chowder. Eat, Terence. Eat. Just try. You've got to stay healthy so you can get better. I count the calories he consumes in one day: 210.

Every day he swallows a Sutent pill. Every day I look for signs that it is starting to work. Every day he seems a little weaker, a little more confused.

"Roll to the left," I say one morning.

He rolls to the right.

"No, sweetie. The LEFT," I say, trying to hold back my irritation. I'm in a hurry for something. For what? I no longer have any idea.

He looks puzzled. I nudge him in the right direction. Something seems odd.

Terry notices it too.

"Mom? Is Dad okay in the head?" he asks me one afternoon.

"I'm not sure," I say.

With his question, I think about what I've been pushing to the back of my brain, that what I have considered Terence's exhaustion may have suddenly changed into something else. This is the first time I've thought of it directly. I am still ignorant of what it means. And odd as it seems, I stay ignorant.

So why can't my mind go there?

Why can't I say the word "die"? Why can't I even think it?

Several years later, I consider my thoughts about my father, who died two years before Terence.

I think about how for years, without being really aware of it, I carried an imaginary picture of what my father's last days would be like. In my mind we sit on a rise in the sunny backyard of the Victorian house where he and my mother have lived for forty-seven years. Deep purple clematis twine around the trellis nearby. The sun is warm, but the air is chilly. His legs are covered with a plaid cashmere blanket. In my imagination, he is in a rattan wheelchair, very FDR. In this picture, Daddy doesn't talk much. He has never talked much. But from time to time he tells me something about what it was like in the Azores, where he was stationed during the war.

What really happened was nothing like that. Instead, on April 20, 2005, my mother left the house to run an errand. Daddy went upstairs to nap. When Mum returned, one look at the bare foot poking out from under the covers and she realized he was gone.

After Terence dies I come to understand that I have also carried a fantasy about how he and I would end our days together. My mental picture is of a hospital bed—we have spent so much time in hospitals the image is burned in my brain. My imaginary dying Terence lies slightly raised. Beside the bed, a tape recorder plays Dixieland, the volume turned down low. We have a tape for each of the children's arrival into our lives—Vivaldi for Terry, Holst's *The Planets* for Georgia—so my imagination supplies a tape for Terence's leaving. Sitting beside the imaginary hospital bed, I read him poetry—Ginsberg, his favorite. Cavafy, mine. Finally we settle on Wordsworth, which we both like. We talk softly about the things we remember.

In this fantasy, as with the one about my dad, one thing is very clear: Everyone in the picture recognizes that the end is near. Something has announced to us that death is approaching and, in my fantasy, we are living out a movie-set version of what should happen.

So when the end actually comes, I can't recognize it as the end of his life. As potent as the signs seem now in retrospect, it just doesn't announce itself as the end of his life. Somehow I manage to see it as just one more crisis to get past. I don't see death because it doesn't look like what I imagine death to look like.

Yet months after it actually happens, I realize that it all unfolded just exactly as I had imagined it.

Except for the part that doesn't.

25

On Friday, December 7, 2007, just as the aide is packing to leave, Terence looks up, startled. The corners of his mouth foam bright red with blood.

"Get him to the emergency room," Dr. Flaherty's nurse, Gloria, says when I call.

I fumble through the telephone book. I know—from our previous experience—that if I call 911, the rescue team will take me only to the closest hospital. I want to get Terence across town to our own hospital, the one at the University of Pennsylvania. The one where Dr. Flaherty works. I pick an emergency service at random from the phone book. The ambulance that arrives is battered and old, the emergency workers scruffy, barely shaven. They struggle with the seated stretcher. I can hear them swallow curses at our narrow stairs. I climb into the ambulance beside Terence. The floor is rusted. There is grime in the corners.

In the emergency room it is clear something is seriously wrong.

"What's your name?" asks the ER doctor. Terence responds correctly.

"What's the date?"

Terence gives the doctor his habitual "Just how dumb are you?" look. But he can't answer.

"Who's the president of the United States?" That triggers something.

"That moron Bush," he says.

I see the numbers on the oxygen monitor above his head drop. Ninety-nine. Ninety-five. Eighty-six. Seventy-eight. The oxygen begins to flow through a tube, and his numbers rise again. That's better. This can be fixed. We have to keep him well. We've got to keep him well long enough for the Sutent to kick in, I tell the emergency room doctor.

I can read the inner dialogue on the physician's face.

One of *those*.

He has never heard of Sutent. I might as well say "unobtanium." I can hear the doctor's thoughts: I have a very sick man here, one who doesn't know the date and whose oxygen levels are dropping precipitously, he is thinking.

And *she's* waiting for a magic pill.

Hours pass. Terence grows querulous.

"I want a Coke," he says. "I want a Coke."

Is surgery ahead? Is a crisis looming? The doctor won't risk filling Terence with liquid. We dip a sponge in Coke and wet his lips with it. Terence gets angrier.

"I want a Coke," he demands. "I want a Coke."

At 10:04 p.m. Terence is admitted to the intensive care ward, where Dr. Eric Goren is doing his last intensive care overnight shift of a three-year residency.

It is here in a break room on the intensive care floor of the University of Pennsylvania hospital in the hours between midnight and dawn that this twenty-nine-year-old not-quite-doctor and I stand beside vending machines selling soft drinks and chips and square off for the battle that is at the core of end-of-life decisions all over the world: Is this, in fact, the end of Terence's life? Neither Dr. Goren nor I yet know the real outcome: that this will be a relatively short skirmish. Later, looking back, I will realize once again that the way I feel at this moment is one of the keys to the end-of-life debate: I still honestly don't believe that it's the final battle. Despite the overwhelming evidence, I believe only that we are facing long odds. Not hopeless odds.

The picture in my head is not of an increasingly gruesome fight over the empty shell of a person. My picture ends with Terence rising from his hospital bed, fragile and frayed perhaps, but back to his old self. In my mind, this is still a temporary crisis that ends with his getting back to something like normal. I am not pushing Sutent on him thinking of how many days it will buy him.

I am thinking weeks. Months. Years.

Even here. Even now. *I still do not see this as an end-of-life battle because I still do not see it as the end of Terence's life.*

On one side of that small break room, Dr. Goren sees a man who is dying. Perhaps tonight. In the other corner, I still see hope ahead.

We negotiate.

Dr. Goren is gentle but blunt. The tiny bubbles of blood are a warning: A "sentinel bleed" he calls it. At any moment this bleeding can, without warning, become uncontrollable. Without my permission to desist, if this happens he will be forced to trigger a full-scale rescue effort.

"It is horrific," he says. "It is ugly and painful. It is not something we want families to see. It is not something you want to see. It is not something even we want to see."

Do you want us to do it? he asks.

Our Sutent experiment is only twenty-two days old, I say. It took Avastin four months to work. Perhaps the new drug still needs more time to kick in. I want to talk to Dr. Flaherty. I can't find him. It is a weekend. He's not around. Dr. Goren and I leave messages. At Dr. Flaherty's office. At his answering service. With the oncologist on call at his office. He's not answering. Where is he? I want to give Sutent a chance. Until I talk to Dr. Flaherty, I don't want to give up.

We settle on what the hospital calls Code-A: Do everything possible to prevent a major bleed or anything life threatening. Don't take heroic measures if death seems inevitable.

Two years later, I track Dr. Goren down. He is still at the University of Pennsylvania, now as an assistant professor of clinical medicine. As I look back on that evening, I now see myself as stubborn and unreasonable, I tell him. Today, I see my refusal to see death in Terence's face as a kind of temporary insanity. Was I insane? Was I outrageous?

Not at all, he answers. You were typical. Absolutely typical, he says. Maybe even a little more reasonable than many. He is now a full-fledged doctor, with two more years of experience. Just in the previous month, he tells me, he presided over the seventh intensive care admission of an elderly woman with Alzheimer's. Over and over she dies, and the family keeps bringing her back to life. The family cannot bear to let her go. The family will not let her go. When death wins it will be only once it breaks through the human shield they form before their mother, their sister, their wife, their grandmother.

Back in the intensive care ward sometime after midnight I call the children in. Georgia is spending the night at a friend's house. My sister picks her up. Terry is at a party. His friends Suzie, Ben, and Will drive him over. Things have changed, I tell Georgia and Terry. We are doing everything we can to save him. But things have changed.

Dad may die tonight.

I say the words because I have to. But they are still just words to me.

. . .

For the next two days, Terence alternates between darkness and light. He is polite but vague when he sees the children.

"Is there something you'd like to say to them?" I ask at one point.

He looks puzzled.

"...No...?"

"Mom, stop leading the witness," Terry chides.

Terence still wants a Coke.

The night nurse is firm. "Mr. Foley, we can't let you drink anything right now. Maybe later..."

Terence smiles sweetly and nods. The charming Professor Foley has entered the room. I can see the bow tie bloom atop his hospital gown. He thanks her. She exits. Instantly, his face contorts in fury. He whips around toward me.

"GO GET IT!" he hisses. "NOW." The Terence I know is still in there. Somewhere.

As morning comes I sleep a bit in a chair, covering myself with my navy raincoat. I awake and Terence is saying strange things.

"That was a swell banquet!" he exclaims at one point. "The cats are here," he says at another moment.

Yet when his friend Dick Epstein arrives, Terence brightens. Dick Epstein, his cable-car-driving, political-fight antagonist, Russia-traveling buddy. Something deep in Terence's mind stirs.

"Clarence...," says Dick. The forty-year-old nickname.

"Dickele!" Terence shouts, using his old Yiddish endearment. Little Dickie!

It's the last thing I hear him say.

26

When morning comes on Monday, the scans are showing signs of cancer in Terence's brain, along with a cascade of hundreds of tiny strokes. I have Terence's signed living will, but I don't need it.

I know what this man who lives for books, music, and ideas would want.

Dr. Flaherty arrives at last. He looks pale.

"I didn't expect this," he says. "I'm sorry."

Together we agree that whatever promise Sutent once held, it holds it no longer. I accept that this is the end, I tell him. He nods. He leaves.

The discussion now shifts to hospice. Hospice is intended for those whose lives will likely last six months or less. Intellectually I grasp that fact. Emotionally, I still do not. Even now, I am planning on a future for us together. A sad future, but a future nonetheless.

The hospital has a hospice program that is administered in the same room where Terence is now lying. The services will change, but he will not need to be moved. Yet the hospital is all the way across the city from our home.

"Are there options for us closer to home?" I ask. "And what about after the six months end?" I am being practical, considering the weeks and months of daily visits that I expect the children and I will be making.

The hospice staff must be used to these discussions. They give me names of places nearer to our neighborhood, and of long-term-care facilities. I am still mentally pushing "the end" out into a distant future. I do not want to see that the end is upon us. Even now, my mind and my gut are at war.

My mind wins. Terence is comfortable in his hospital bed. I leave him there. We can move him later, I reason. On Tuesday, December 11, 2007, at 1:18 p.m., I sign the papers that turn the bed in which he lies from hospital to hospice. The hospital staff takes away the machines and the monitors. They remove the oxygen tubes. They silence the steady click of the heart monitor. The green wiggly lines above his head go dark. The oncologists and radiologists and lab technicians disappear. Another group of people—hospice nurses, social workers, chaplains, and counselors—appear, to help Terence, me, and the children. The focus shifts from treating Terence to easing his transition. And ours.

A chaplain stops by to pray with us. She and I chat. She confesses that she does not much like her work. It leaves her exhausted and hopeless. I can see your point, I say. Another woman, a registered nurse named Jennifer, comes by twice a day. Jennifer is the death specialist. She explains to me what is going on, what each of the medications is, and what Terence may be experiencing.

For the next three days, Terence lies still in the same hospital bed. Over those three days, we spend $14,022, less than a third of the previous four days' $43,711. What costs $14,000? Our last car? It is a dowdy two-year-old gold Sable. A year at a state college? Here it buys a bed, the pain and anxiety medications Ativan and Dilaudid, monitoring for him, and counseling, a different kind of pain management for the children and me.

I accept that Terence is dying. Even now, I still can't fathom it. When he drifts into a coma, I beg the nurse to reduce the medications so he will wake up again.

It isn't the medicine, she explains. "He has begun the dying process," she says.

Still, to humor me, she reduces the dose. Terence begins to fidget, to pick at the bedclothes. His face, previously peaceful, contorts in some unseen discomfort. Yet he does not awaken. Okay, I say, put it back. Jennifer's records show that I "verbalized understanding."

Verbalized, yes.

Understanding?

Still not quite.

And so here it is at last, just as I now realize I had imagined it all along.

Sun streams through the window. His old black cassette recorder is by the bed. The South Frisco band is playing. The jaunty two-beat music that once filled our house is now filling the hospital room.

And here I am beside the bed, reading to him just as I imagined. What is missing from this scene as I once fantasized it?

Terence.

It's not Wordsworth I am reading. Not "The Ruined Abbey." Not "Howl." No. It is his friends' good-byes that I am reading. And mine. Together, Terence and I have pushed the bell curve as far as we are able. We have skated so close to the thin ice of probabilities that, in the end, we have crashed through. I am still here to say good-bye to him. He is no longer able to say good-bye to me.

Still, I press on. Surely the Terence I know is big enough, and fierce enough and robust enough—surely there is some of that Terence somewhere inside this sleeping man. I email his friends around the world and read their responses to him. Layers of his life unfold before me as I fill the room with their voices. Cousin

Margo says good-bye, I say. My mind calls up the 1950s snapshot of Margo, her two brothers, and Terence on the cement steps of her parents' bungalow. She is like a little sister to him. Good-bye, says Margo. Good-bye from all of us, from Cousin Glenn and from Miles and Jane. Uncle Fred, the eldest of Terence's half brothers, floats in the room speaking for the other three boys, the family lost and found. Good-bye Terence, good-bye from your brothers. Aunt Rita, the half sister so nearly his own age, speaks through me: I wish we had known you better, Terence, she says. Good-bye. Good-bye. The hours roll on. The sun moves past and shadows fill the room. One by one his friends check in. One by one, I use words to welcome in images of the friends of his life-time.

"It's Spider," I say to Terence, Steve Stryder, his high school buddy. Spider is saying good-bye. Good-bye to high school. And trumpet. And long beer-filled evenings. Good-bye Woody Boyd, Pat Blackwell, and the Philippines. Pat sends snapshots of their long-ago sailor selves. Once again in the shadows I spin in this hospital room, Terence and Woody and Patrick goof around. They pick up girls. They fight the last war—and the next—in their heads as they sit on a curb by the sea.

From Vermont, Charly Dickerson says good-bye. A week from now he will say at the funeral how he and Terence became friends—in prison, where they both worked, believing they could transform even the worst. Good-bye from Charly. Good-bye from Mardean. Good-bye from the whole crowd up there who still be-lieve that bad can become good and justice and redemption are right around the corner. Good-bye from Vermont. Good-bye from Sean Delgrosso, the Beijing friend who stood up for Ter-ence at our wedding, crisp in his Marine dress blues. Good-bye from Sean, I whisper. I fill the tiny room with the ghostly layers of his life. Dan Metraux. Joel Gross. Linda Kamal. Good-bye, Ter-ence. They all say good-bye.

The good-byes he would have said had he been able I now say for him, to all his friends, his family, his children. Every day for three days I speak to him of the kids and for the kids. And of me. And us. I tell him private things, things I want him to hear. Things I know he knows. I sleep in a chair by his side.

At about 2:30 a.m. Friday, a noise in the hall startles me. I awake just in time to hold his hand as he dies.

A doctor enters. It is 2:44 a.m. Terence is now pronounced officially dead. She departs and everything becomes still. His friends' images leave the room. One by one the voices I conjured recede. The doctors are gone. The nurses are gone. Now Terence too is gone. I sit quietly for a moment. Can I feel him anywhere? Is there anything left of him in this room? There is nothing. The room is silent. There is only me left. I gather up my things and take an elevator downstairs.

I walk through the deserted lobby, hail a cab in the dark, and head home alone.

Afterward

Ten days later, the kids hang Daddy's Christmas stocking along-side our three. I mail the cards he had addressed months earlier, slipping in a black-bordered note. I throw away the protein bars, give the energy drinks to a shelter, and wash an opened bottle of Sutent down the drain.

For years, Terence used to tell a story, almost certainly apocryphal, about his uncle Bob. Climbing aboard a landing craft before the invasion of Normandy, so the story went, Bob's sergeant told the men that by the end of the day, nine out of ten would be dead. Said Bob, on hearing that news: "Each one of us looked around and felt so sorry for those other nine poor sonsabitches."

Did Terence know that we would be in that same boat?

For months after Terence dies, the kids and I struggle with the sense of unreality. I keep his cellphone in my purse until I frighten the children by accidentally pocket-calling them from his number. We all do double-takes at the sight of a familiar hat or jacket, the sight of his grin in a crowd.

"Sometimes I feel that Dad is just really hard to reach right now," Terry says.

I frighten myself by developing an inexplicable compulsion: All day, every day, I frantically refresh my email. The habit is getting in the way of my work—until a therapist helps me realize what I am doing: I am looking for the email that never comes. I am looking for the message from Terence saying he is coming back home. In a strange echo of my inability to believe he was dying, I can't quite believe he is dead.

We bury Terence at St. Peter's Church, in a sunny spot right outside the church door. Once a week I walk the six blocks from our house, sit on the stone, and tell him the news. Georgia made the honor roll. Terry's band has a new CD. That shortcut to the highway? You were right. It's faster. Georgia went to Brazil. Terry changed schools. The kids took me out for Mother's Day. That lunatic neighbor? He moved.

Slowly, slowly we all emerge from the black hole. Our friends and family step in to ease the void. Georgia draws and writes and confides in her friends. Terry becomes the musician that his dad dreamed of. More Christmases go by. Terence's old friends stay my friends; our cousins become our extended family.

And eventually, I fall in love again.

In love with a man as kind and loving, as smart and funny, and as generous and quirky as any who has ever walked this earth.

Not a day goes by that I don't wish back the days and years that Terence lost with me and his family. Nor, paradoxically, does a day go by when I am not amazed and grateful for this new love, and this new life. A partner for me. A friend for my children, just as I am a friend to his. I think about that long-ago day in Kentucky when, facing what he thought was his imminent death, Terence's first thought was of how best to protect and comfort me. Another gift, I think. The gift of being able to love again.

As I look back, I wonder: Is there anything I would have done differently? I am sad that Terence and I worked so hard to save him that we never gave ourselves time to say good-bye. But when should we have conceded he was dying? From the very first, when we learned he had a rare and aggressive disease? When the metastases gave him, statistically, only months to live? When the cancer began its renewed march? At which one of these moments—each of which presented itself to us as possibly the end—would it have been better for us to concede defeat?

No, sad as I am at our silent farewell, I would not trade away any of those years of fighting for life.

I set out to find out the cost of Terence's care and of the drugs that may or may not have prolonged his life. I secretly hoped to find out something else. Did I do the right thing?

I'm not sure I found the answer to that question, or that I ever will.

What I found instead was the cost of our hope. Was that hope good for us? Without question. For us the fight for life, with all its frustration, confusion, and failure, changed what should have been the seven most dismal years of our lives into the seven most wonderful.

Yet our quest cost so much more than I believe it should have, and that expense put that hope far beyond the reach of too many others.

Perhaps, I think, I have found at least part of the answer in a place I at first didn't realize I was looking. Perhaps the answer— or a piece of it—lies in the most mundane details of our journey. What if Terence and I were able to see more clearly some of the costs of the procedure? Would we have been able to make wiser choices? Less expensive choices? Even choices that might have made better sense for us?

I believe we would have forgone the painful and ineffective IL-2 treatment because we would have had to think harder about it. As long as it was free—which it was, to us—Terence almost had to seize on even the tiniest possibility that it could help.

And what if there were a system in which we could see the

prices for the scans—would Terence have had seventy-six of them? Was each and every one of them equally necessary to his care? Were some of them even harmful? Could we perhaps have even been better off for having had slightly less treatment, for having spent slightly less money?

And yet without bigger changes in the way health care is paid for and delivered, how would even that lead to a fairer way of sharing the access to medical care—so that I with my good health insurance don't take everything, leaving you with nothing? Right now, if we choose to skip some expensive treatment that has only a minuscule chance of success, what effect will that have on you? None. It may save some money for my employer—a reasonable goal, of course—but it won't help you get some kind of treatment that you might need.

What can we do about a system in which neither the people who pay—our employers—nor the people who use the services—Terence and I and everyone like us—can really see or influence the cost?

A system in which prices are set as in a giant Chinese bazaar? A system in which $600,000 in bills becomes $200,000 in payments, and as much as possible of the cost of care for people who can't or won't pay their bills is tucked into the negotiating space between those numbers?

And what can we do about a system that is so maddeningly complex to navigate? One that took days, weeks, months, even whole years of our lives to figure out? One that leaves me, even today, four years after Terence's death, not entirely sure we did the right thing? Why was this system designed for the doctors, hospitals, laboratories, and technicians and not for Terence and me? What if the doctors in the hospital and the oncologist who treated Terence had been on the same team? What if they had been talking to one another rather than having their debate about Terence's prospects only through me?

Would we all have been better off?

Would we all have made better and more rational choices? I think so.

And what about the choices themselves?

I discovered that death does not always arrive in an easily recognizable form. To call it "denial"—this inability of ours to see, and acknowledge, death stalking our loved ones—is to almost laughably understate its force. Clearly knowing in advance the wishes of our loved ones is key. Yet it is almost certainly not enough. Terence and I had both signed legal documents clearly stating our preferences. We knew that neither of us would want to push on past the inevitable. Yet neither of us could clearly see the inevitable until it was absolutely unavoidable.

Since more than a quarter of all medical care is provided in the last two years of life, surely we must come up with a better way of helping ease families to gentler—and less costly—transitions.

But where would this help come from? I also learned that there are no true bystanders. The system masks all kinds of agendas—personal, professional, financial. Everyone in the process—doctors, nurses, hospitals, pathologists, me, Terence—has some stake in the outcome. Hospitals are paid only for what they do, not for what they don't do. The doctors want to cure, to succeed, to practice their craft, to make a good living, to save a patient. Many are consultants to the drug companies, which in turn want their drugs to succeed.

Surely we all could be helped by someone standing outside this process who could ease us through our decision-making, who could help us understand and be more dispassionate about what we are facing.

For all the system's flaws, there is so much about it that is amazing—that as many people as possible should be able to enjoy.

Two years after Terence's death, I wade through a snowstorm to Keith Flaherty's office in Boston, where he has moved to a new job that lets him intensify his work on the kind of targeted therapy he used with Terence.

Together, Dr. Flaherty and I look at the numbers—the result of the Avastin/Nexavar clinical trial. The average patient in his trial got fourteen months of extra life. Dr. Flaherty estimates that, without any treatment, someone at Terence's stage of the disease would live three months. Terence got seventeen months—still within the realm of chance but way, way up on the bell curve.

There's another bell curve that starts about where Terence's left off. It charts the survival times for patients treated not just with Sutent, Avastin, and Nexavar but also with Afinitor and Votrient—drugs made available within the past three years. Doctors and patients now are doing what we dreamed of, staggering one drug after another and buying years more of life.

At the 2008 meeting of the American Society of Clinical Oncology, Dr. Flaherty presented the results of the clinical trial that Terence was part of. The slides and charts showed the other cancer doctors that Avastin and Nexavar work well on a wide variety of patients.

Yet of all the people who saw those slides, only Dr. Flaherty and I know that the solitary tick mark at seventeen months was Terence.

Only I know that those seventeen months include an afternoon looking down at the Mediterranean with Georgia from a sunny balcony in southern Spain. Moving Terry into his college dorm. Celebrating our twentieth anniversary with a carriage ride through Philadelphia's cobbled streets. That final Thanksgiving game of charades with cousins Margo and Glenn. And one last chance for Terence to pave the way for someone else—or, as he might have said, for all those other poor sonsabitches.

ACKNOWLEDGMENTS

This book grew out of an article published by Bloomberg News and *Bloomberg Businessweek* on March 4, 2010. I would like to express my appreciation to everyone at Bloomberg for the opportunity to expand the work into this book, and most especially to editor in chief Matt Winkler.

I benefited enormously from the editorial skills of my Bloomberg colleagues, who edited, reported, nudged, critiqued, and suggested. These include Bob Blau, Reg Gale, Bob Ivry, Norm Pearlstine, Shannon Pettypiece, Ellen Pollock, Anne Reifenberg, Marybeth Sandell, Bob Simison, Josh Tyrangiel, Mike Waldholz, and Ken Wells. I owe special thanks to my colleague Chuck Babcock, whose investigative skills I leaned on so heavily in sorting through the piles of complex documents. And to Reto Gregori, who makes everything happen, everywhere, all the time.

Thanks to all my wonderful friends, family, and colleagues who read, commented on, and corrected my manuscript: Sandra Mims Rowe, John Carroll, Nikhil Deogun, Doug Blackmon, Chuck Camp, Rebecca Blumenstein, Sharon Luckerman, Sidney Rittenberg, Joan Maxwell, Abbe Fletman, Jane Hinkle, Dick and Barbara Epstein, Woody and Sandra Boyd, Charly Dickerson and Mardean Moglein, Fred and Gail Laudeman, Bill Laudeman, Dick Laudeman, Charles Laudeman, Rita Brown, Margo and Glenn Lindahl, and Miles Lindahl. Special thanks to Jane Lindahl, whose editorial assistance got me through; to my sister Alix Bennett, who always gets me through, and her daughters, Aly and Greylin; and to my mother, my brother Peter, and my sister Kathryn.

All of the doctors involved in Terence's care were amazingly thoughtful and generous with their time and insights as I reconstructed their roles in the journey. Thanks to Ronald Bukowski, Keith Flaherty, P. Holbrook Howard, Eric Goren, Allen Gown, Scott Pierce, and Craig Turner.

This wouldn't have been a book at all without Amanda Urban, my wonderful agent; Kate Medina at Random House, who is the kind of editor that hardly exists anymore; and Lindsey Schwoeri, who is becoming that kind of editor too.

Then there's Don, and our improbably wonderful next chapter. And of course Terry and Georgia, who have always been the reason for everything, for both me and their dad.

PERMISSIONS

Much of the medical and cost material first appeared in articles in Bloomberg News and in *Businessweek* on March 4, 2010. These articles can be found here:

"Lessons of a $618,616 Death"
http://www.businessweek.com/magazine/content/10_11
/b4170032321836.htm

"End-of-Life Warning at $618,616 Makes Me Wonder Was It Worth It"
http://www.bloomberg.com/apps/news?pid=newsarchive&sid=
avRFGNF6Qw_w

In addition, I draw extensively on the work of three Bloomberg colleagues: Chuck Babcock, Ken Wells, and Shannon Pettypiece. I depended heavily on Chuck's March 4, 2010, Bloomberg articles on interpreting the cost of medications ("Avastin Dose Costing $6,600 Became $27,360 in Hospital Billing," http://www.bloomberg.com/apps/news?pid=newsarchive&sid=aXuekMxp5Yh4) and of scans ("Chest Scan Costs $550 to $3,232 in Opaque Market for Radiology," http://www.bloomberg.com/apps/news?pid=news archive&sid=auQxUuJ1.Srk), as well as on Ken and Shannon's article on the development of Sutent and other targeted therapies ("Miracle Cancer Drug Extends Life with $48,720 Cost," http://www.bloomberg.com /apps/news?pid=newsarchive&sid=aER.9zj2HmSk). Ken's detailed interviews with Dr. Keith Flaherty were also invaluable.

I gratefully acknowledge Bloomberg's permission to use this material.

ABOUT THE AUTHOR

AMANDA BENNETT is an executive editor at Bloomberg News, directing special projects and investigations, and was the co-chair of the Pulitzer Prize Board. She formerly served as editor of *The Philadelphia Inquirer,* editor of the *Herald-Leader* (Lexington, Kentucky), managing editor for *The Oregonian* (Portland, Oregon), and Atlanta bureau chief (among numerous other posts) at *The Wall Street Journal.* In 1997 Bennett shared the Pulitzer Prize for national reporting with her *Journal* colleagues, and in 2001 she led an *Oregonian* team to a Pulitzer for public service. She is the author of previous books including *In Memoriam* (1997), *The Man Who Stayed Behind* (1993), and *The Death of the Organization Man* (1990).